WROUGHT

IRON

DESIGNS

Published by Artistic Ironworkers Supplies Ltd, Kidderminster DY10 1HT.

ISBN 0 9511949 0 9

Introduction

This book of 1/10 scale drawings has been produced for fabricators and designers as a simple guide and, we hope, inspiration on how to use our supplies of ready formed 'wrought iron' pattern modules.

Our handbook 'Wrought iron art' fully illustrates, and dimensions, the individual modules, which is very necessary information for the designer and fabricator. This book is complementary to it and is a visual aid to demonstrate how the modules can be combined to achieve different styles, and densities of pattern. An important point to remember when using this book is that the designs are meant to depict concepts that can be reproduced as gates, grilles, fencing etc. by using part of or multiples of the design. Thus a concept design could be repeated vertically to double the height and/or extended horizontally virtually indefinitely. Our biggest problem in compiling and selecting these designs was to try to include schemes to suit all tastes and at varying cost levels, when to contain all the possibilities would run to many volumes. May we leave it to you and your artistic imagination to compile the remainder?

Design Considerations

The first consideration when designing a scheme using repeating modules of a set size is that of dimensional flexibility for the outer framework. This can be achieved in a number of ways.

1. By cropping marginal modules to produce required finished frame sizes.

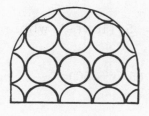

FIG.1

2. By introducing space between 'blocks' of modules. It is then possible for both width and height of framework to be infinitely varied.

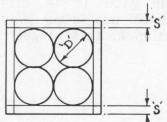 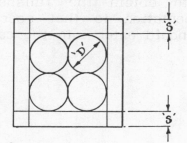 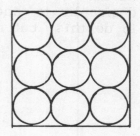

where 2S is less than 'D'   where 2S is less than 'D'   where 2S = 'D'

FIG.2   FIG.3   FIG.4

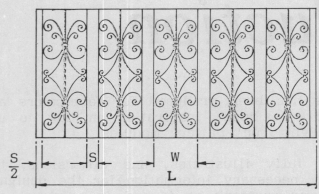

$$\frac{S}{2} \quad \quad S \quad \quad W$$

$$L$$

$$W$$

FIG.5

BASIC ROUTE TO 'SPACE' DETERMINATION

How many modules? $M = \dfrac{L}{W}$ (lowest whole number)

How much total space? $TS = L - M \times W$

How many spaces? = same number as modules

Size of each space? $S = \dfrac{TS}{M}$

Working Example

L = 2000

W = 350

How many modules? $M = \dfrac{2000}{350} = 5$ (lowest whole number)

How much space? $TS = 2000 - (5 \times 350)$

$$TS = 250$$

Size of each space? $S = \dfrac{250}{5} = 50$

Having created space to obtain the finished frame size it is often
desirable to add ornamentation to that space. There are many ways
to do this, but design should enter into the consideration at this stage.

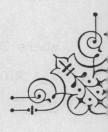

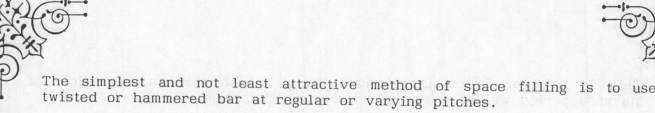

The simplest and not least attractive method of space filling is to use twisted or hammered bar at regular or varying pitches.

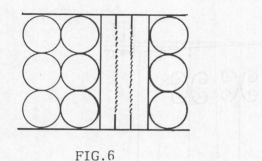

FIG.6

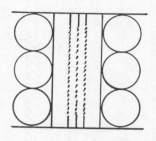

FIG.7

The size of the bar should ideally be proportionate to the materials used in the pattern module. Some typical matchings would be

e.g. scroll material size 16 x 4mm - use twisted bar 16 x 4mm

scroll material size 12 x 6mm - use twisted or hammered bar 12 x 12mm

scroll material size 12 x 12mm - use twisted or hammered bar 14mm Sq.

An alternative and popular way of space filling is to use complementary 'C' or 'S' scrolls. Complementary meaning the same material size and scroll style as the module. These can usually be arranged in groups or singly to give a varying dimension.

Using 'S' scrolls

FIG.8   FIG.9   FIG.10

Using 'C' scrolls

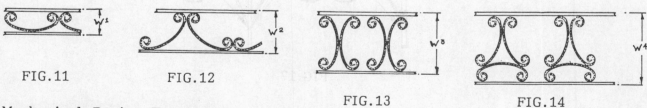

FIG.11   FIG.12

FIG.13   FIG.14

Mechanical Design Factors

Besides looking attractive a wrought iron design should also have, or impart to its framework, sufficient rigidity to prevent the whole from sagging under its own weight.

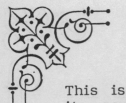

This is an example of an unbraced design which through the effect of its unsupported weight causes parallelogram distortion.

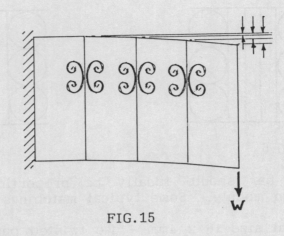

FIG.15

By moving the same scroll pattern to the top of the uprights a series of braced corners are formed to prevent sag.

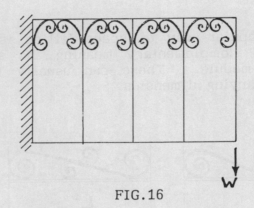

FIG.16

FIG.17

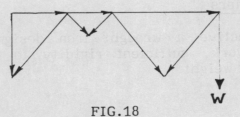

FIG.18

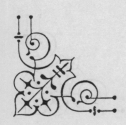

It can be seen how, combining the requirements to size frameworks using 'space', and using scrolls correctly to provide ornamentation in those spaces, you can produce a stressed structure of great artistic appeal.

A border panel of scrolls, surrounding a simple vertical unbraced internal block, will usually provide sufficient bracing whilst the contrary is also true. A panel comprising of an internal block of rosettes, welded at their points of contact produces a highly braced core around which an unstressed frame can be distanced by simple spacers.

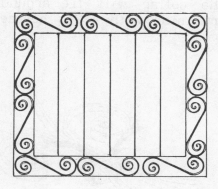

FIG.19

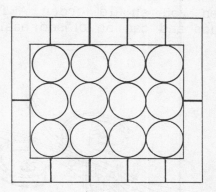

FIG.20

A typical use for the latter format is where a panel of ironwork is to be used in an irregular aperture. For instance, where solid panels or balusters are removed from a wooden staircase and landing it is usually impossible to obtain an exact fit of the iron framework to the woodwork and unsightly, variable gaps are obvious. Making the framework smaller all round and using tabular spacers to fix through means that the eye does not pick up these irregularities.

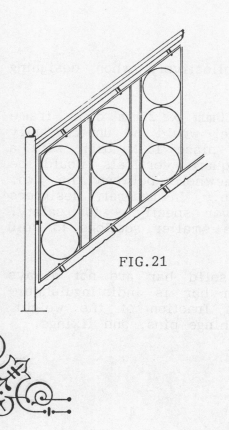

FIG.21

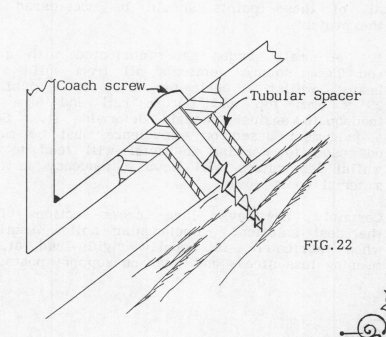

Coach screw

Tubular Spacer

FIG.22

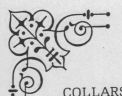

COLLARS OR CLIPS

Many of our modules have collars fitted over the scroll joints to reproduce the traditional style of scroll clipping. We provide a range of ready made collars or straight lengths of collar material so that the complete work can be finished in the same fashion, if so desired. For the better quality work it should be considered essential to use collars in order to mask welded scroll joins. The ready made collars are supplied in a choice of sizes according to the size of scroll material and how many scrolls the collar needs to enclose e.g. if your scroll material is 12 x 6mm and you require to enclose 4 bars of material, then you should order ART 158/16. The collar will fit around three sides and can be closed easily on the fourth side with a 2lb hammer.

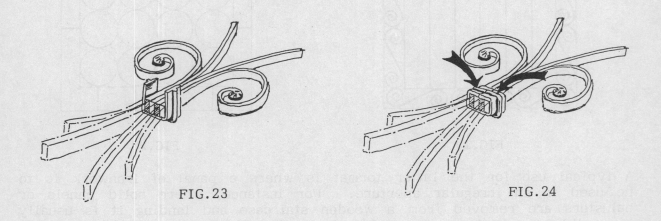

FIG.23   FIG.24

FRAMEWORK

Framework material sizes are dependent on several interrelated factors
1. Application.
2. Appearance.
3. Durability and environment.

All of these points should be considered collectively when designing the project.

1. A small garden gate fabricated with a 50mm x 25mm outer frame and 25mm square verticals all from solid steel would be unnecessarily heavy, whilst a perimeter fence to a public place 1.7M high with a 25 x 6mm top and bottom rail and 8mm square verticals would be inadequate against vandals deforming it. Somewhere between the two, a judgement based on experience must be made. In general, designers not used to working in metal will tend to over specify - for safety, whilst fabricators will have a tendency to the smaller sections to hold material costs down.

Certainly, nowadays, large cross sections of solid bar are not always the best solution. Rectangular hollow section bar is indistinguishable when fabricated, is equally rigid, and at a fraction of the weight, meaning less stress and wear on support posts, hinge pins, and fixings.

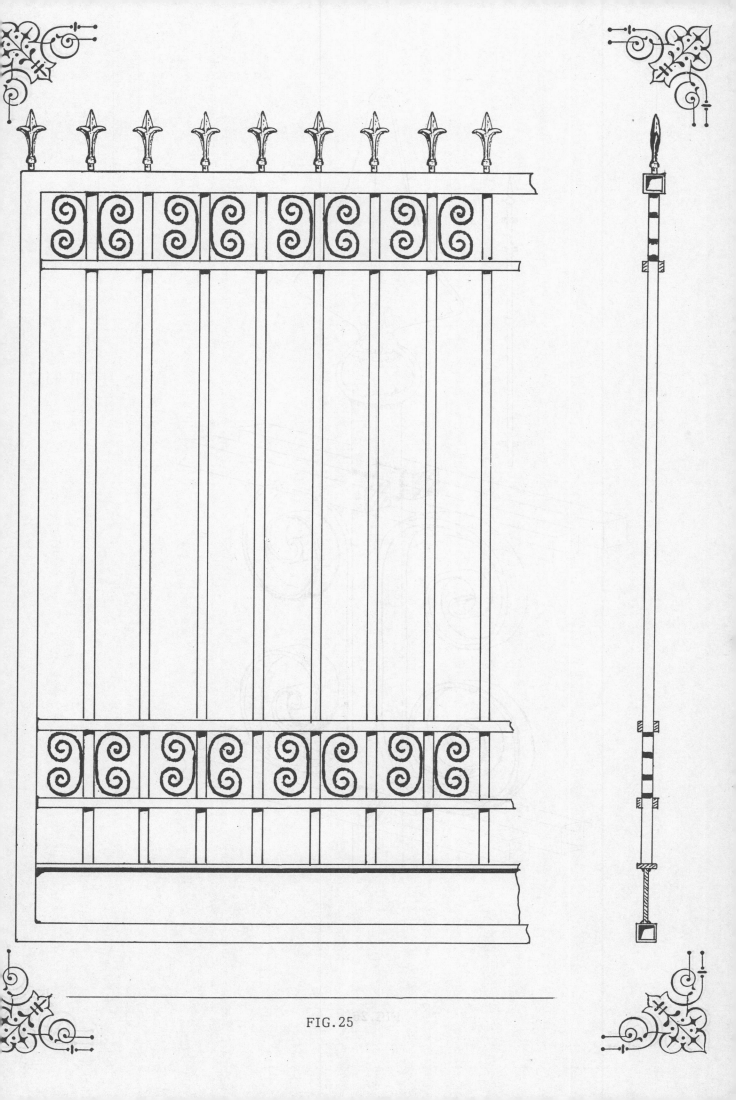

FIG. 25

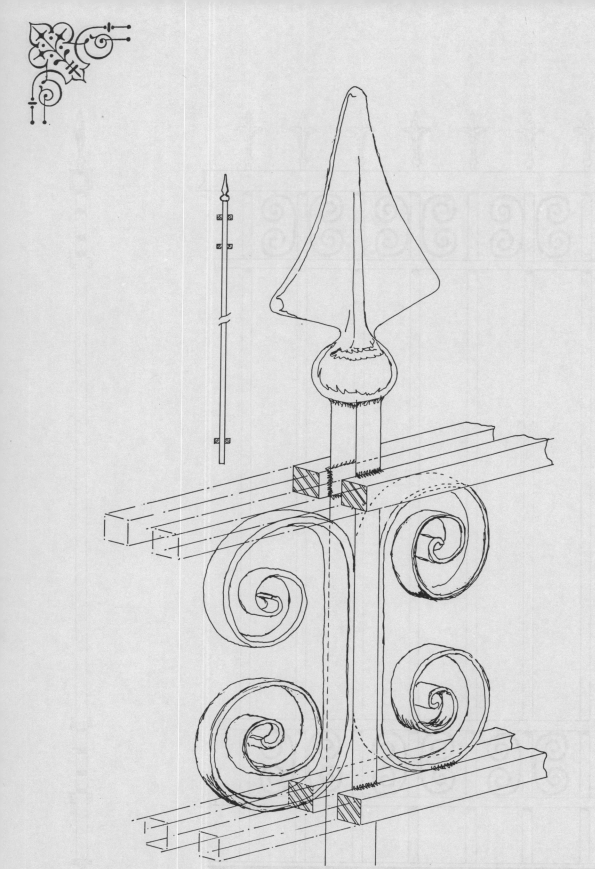

FIG. 26

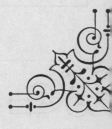

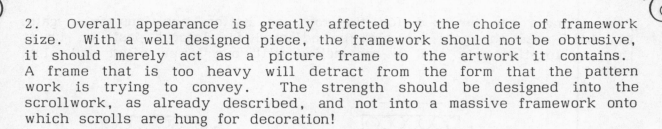

2.   Overall appearance is greatly affected by the choice of framework size. With a well designed piece, the framework should not be obtrusive, it should merely act as a picture frame to the artwork it contains. A frame that is too heavy will detract from the form that the pattern work is trying to convey.   The strength should be designed into the scrollwork, as already described, and not into a massive framework onto which scrolls are hung for decoration!

Framework material sizes should also reflect the durability requirements and must be considered in relation to the location of the work e.g. human traffic density and variety, internal or external work and briny atmospheres etc.

Extra wide unsupported panels can be given added stiffness by the inclusion of a bottom web of steel plate.   A typical cross section of a design that has proved successful on a 4M span unsupported single gate wing is shown in Fig. 25.

Railings

The traditional method of piercing the top and bottom rails of a fence or gate panel to locate the vertical bars is expensive, because of the requirement for a mechanical press to perform the operation on cold metal, or the use of a forge, punches and drifts to perform the operation hot. The usual method adopted now is to weld the vertical bars either side of the rail to create the same appearance but with no detrimental effect. An alternative economical approach, which is very strong and overcomes the aligning problem of welding in separate parts and of piercing the rails is shown in Fig. 26.   The intersection joins are best welded all round to preclude the ingress of water.

FITTINGS & FIXINGS

Wherever possible it is advantageous to make the ironwork demountable for maintenance or repair purposes. Lugs built into brickwork onto which the fence can be bolted allow for this eventuality.   Our adjustable hinges, ideal for heavier gates, not only allow the gates to be aligned correctly they also permit demounting.

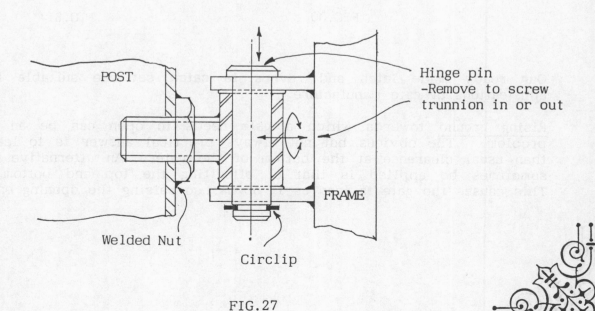

FIG.27

These hinges can be used for the top and bottom positions on a gate, in which case the gate can also be adjusted for lateral position, or at the top location only and in conjunction with our lower pivot and plate sets.

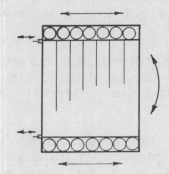

FIG.28

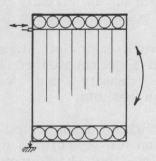

FIG.29

Hinges should, ideally, be set to the furthest distance vertically apart that is practical. This reduces unnecessary leverage loads. Hinges should also be located on or close to a horizontal gate rail so that the hinge style of the gate is not subject to vertical distortion.

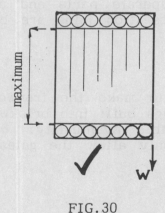

FIG.30

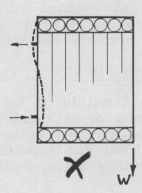

FIG.31

Our ready made latch and reversible catch set are suitable for most applications of gate manufacture.

Rising ground towards which a gate needs to open can be an awkward problem. The obvious but not always practical answer is to leave more than usual clearance at the bottom of the gate. An alternative that can sometimes be applied is that of offsetting the top and bottom hinges. This causes the gate to lean as it opens, so raising the opening end.

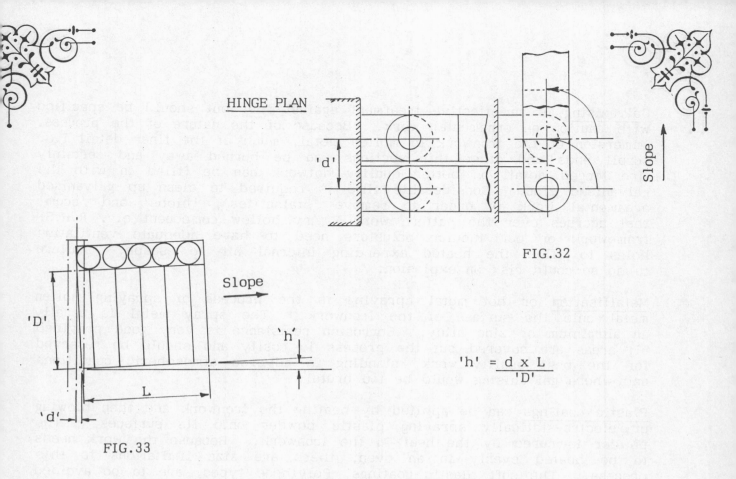

HINGE PLAN

FIG.32

Slope

Slope

$$'h' = \frac{d \times L}{'D'}$$

FIG.33

This feature can also be applied to make a self closing gate.

SURFACE FINISHING METALWORK

INTERIOR

For interior work, paint is the normal surface finish. One coat of good quality metal primer an undercoat and one top coat is usually sufficient. Traditionally, matt black or a white gloss are used. Increasing in favour for the forged quality work is the burnished metal appearance, obtained with a wire brush, and retained by painting with polyurethane clear lacquer. For effect, an overall application of translucent varnish tinted with green or blue and then the features of the ironwork e.g. Baroque leaves, twists and collars highlighted with gold leaf, imparts a degree of luxury to ironwork that is difficult to better. Wrought iron work does not have to be black or white!

EXTERIOR

Modern painting systems are greatly improved, as a result of chemical research, and claims of 5 and 10 years maintenance life, for properly applied paint finishes can be believed.
The overall considerations of the longevity of a paint finish are firstly, rust free metal before application of the primer and secondly, especially with ornamental work, total coverage of the metal surface. The latter, is best achieved, by the total immersion of the work in a 'Dip-Tank'. A second best application method would be by electro-static spraying. Hand painting can be very effective, but is very labour intensive.

Galvanising is an effective treatment against rust but should be specified with caution on ornamental work. Because of the nature of the process, immersion of the ironwork in molten metal, much of the finer detail i.e. scroll ends and other thin sections can be burned away and certainly fine forged detail on better quality hotwork can be filled in with the galvanised zinc. Considerable time is required to clean up galvanised ornamental work in order to remove 'stalactites', 'blobs' and 'scum' that accrues over the pattern work. Any hollow component e.g. R.H.S. framework or our tubular balusters need to have adequate ventilation holes to allow the heated expanding internal air to escape. Failure to do so could risk an explosion.

Metallisation or hot metal spraying is the process of spraying molten metal onto the surface of the ironwork. The spray metal is usually an aluminium or zinc alloy. Corrosion resistance is very good provided all areas are covered but the process is costly and should be reserved for the best quality work, standing in adverse atmospheric conditions and where galvanising would be too brutal.

Plastic coatings can be applied by heating the ironwork and then blowing or electro-statically spraying plastic powder onto its surfaces. The powder is cured by the heat in the ironwork. Because the work needs to be heated evenly in an oven, there are size limitations to this process. The soft plastic coatings, Polythene types, are to be avoided but the harder, thinner Epoxy, Polyester and Nylon types are suitable for some applications, though they tend to be relatively expensive.

Building Regulations

Certain situations, especially balconies and staircases, are sometimes governed by Building Regulations with regard to the height and spacing of balusters. We do not wish to be authoritative on this matter because of the variable factors that can influence the requirements. However, our standard modules can invariably be made to comply, for instance, where a balcony needs to be 1100mm high and our module is supplied at 900mm, the inclusion of a horizontal pattern row will increase the height.

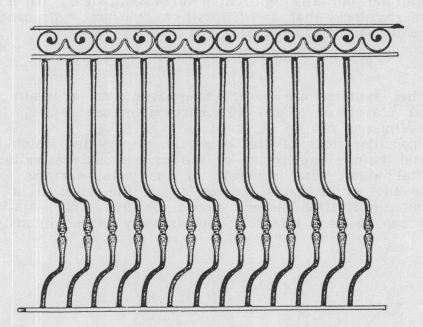

FIG.34

Where a pattern module allows the passage of a 100mm sphere, then the inclusion of an intermediate twisted or hammered bar and/or additional complementary scrolls will close the space.

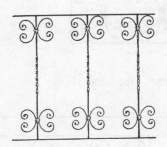

FIG.35

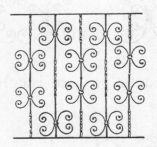

FIG.36

The designs contained in this book are drawn to 1:10 scale unless otherwise stated and are as accurate as the processes used in their production allow. They are not intended as working plans and should not be scaled for that purpose. Whilst every endeavour has been made to ensure accuracy in the information supplied, no responsibility can be admitted by Artistic Ironworkers Supplies Ltd. resulting from the use of this book and its contents.

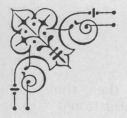
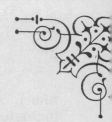

summary

Choose a
pattern module

Add modules

Frame the modules

Make the frame wider

Make the frame higher

Make it stronger

Fill the spaces

Decorate

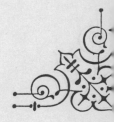

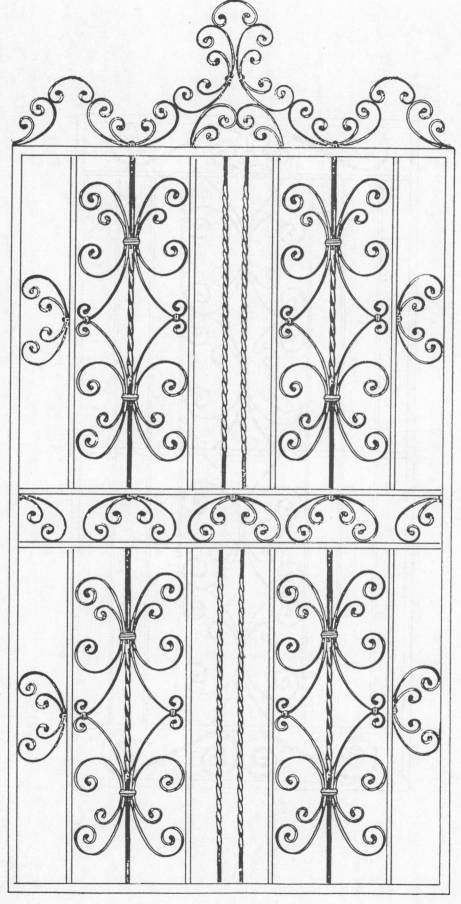

Art 51/3
Art 88/9
Art 88/10
Art 119/23

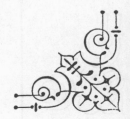

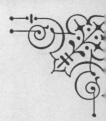

Art 74/3
Art 70/1

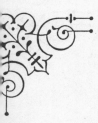

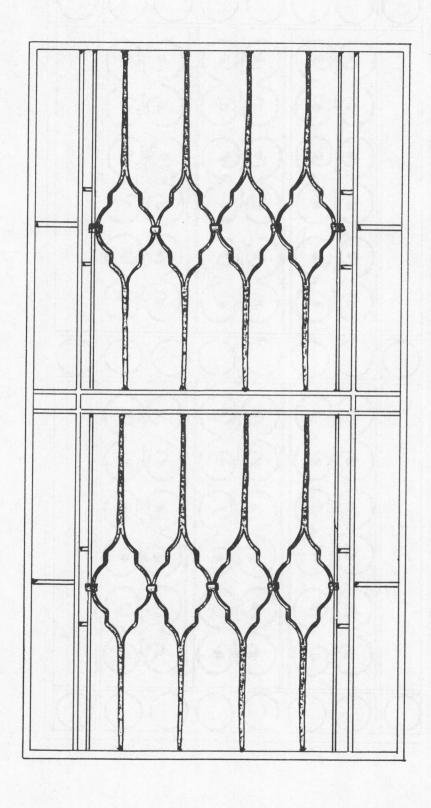

Art 107/1

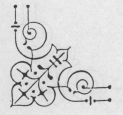

Art 29/1
Art 157/6

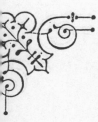

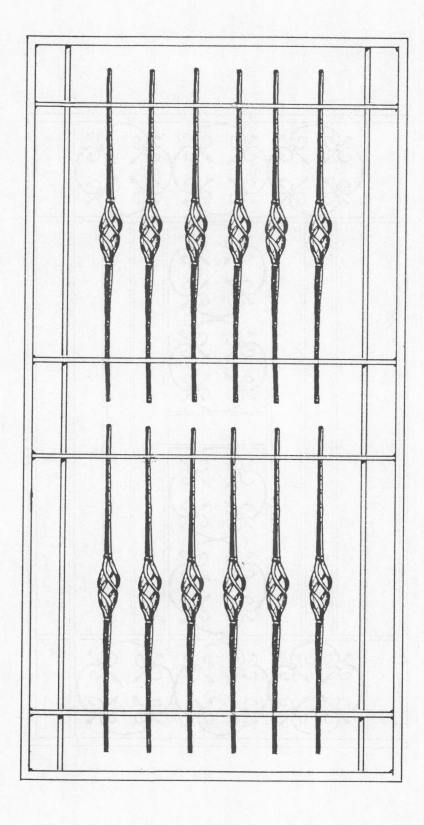

Art 102/1

Art 23/1

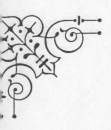

7

Art 103/1
Art 117/7
Art 119/24
Art 120/1

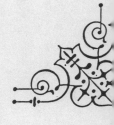

Art 141/1

Art 18/2

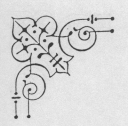
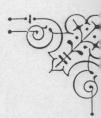
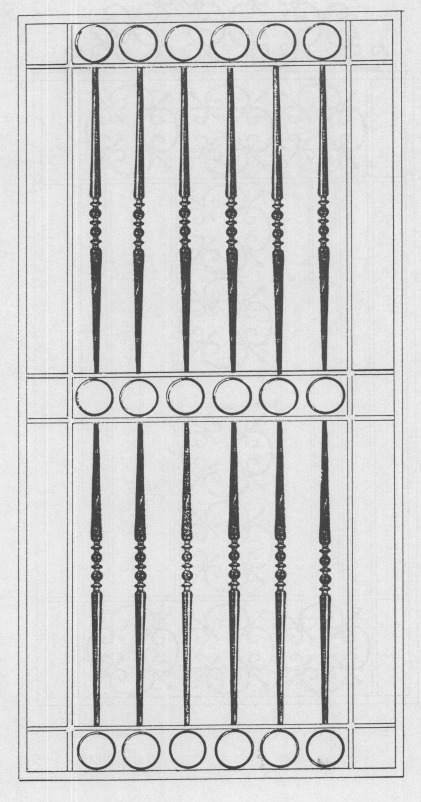
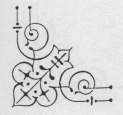

Art 149/2
Art 157/6

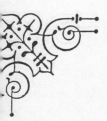

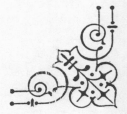

Art 52/2   Art 94/2
Art 93/1   Art 94/3
Art 94/1   Art 119/23

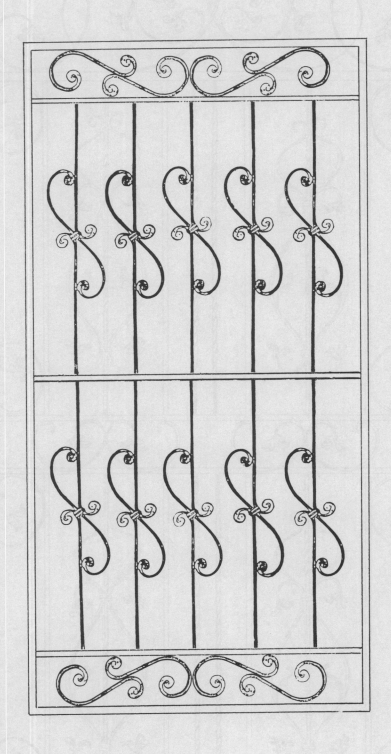

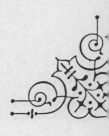

Art 73/2
Art 58/2

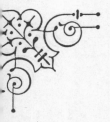

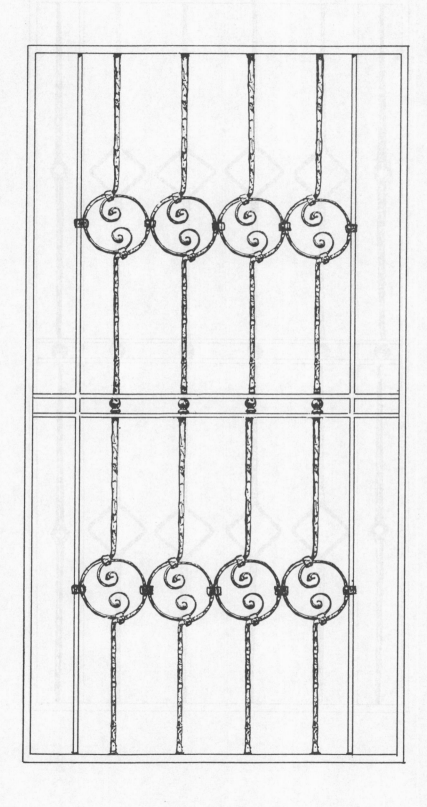

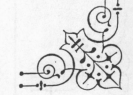

Art 106/1
Art 155/3

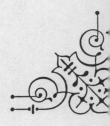

Art 108/2
Art 101/1
Art 117/7

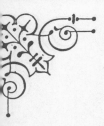

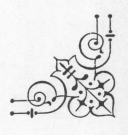

Art 51/3
Art 88/10
Art 119/23

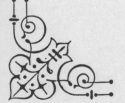

Art 24/1
Art 82/1
Art 90/2

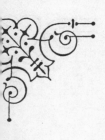
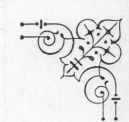

17

Art 24/1
Art 90/2
Art 124/7

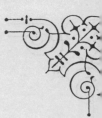

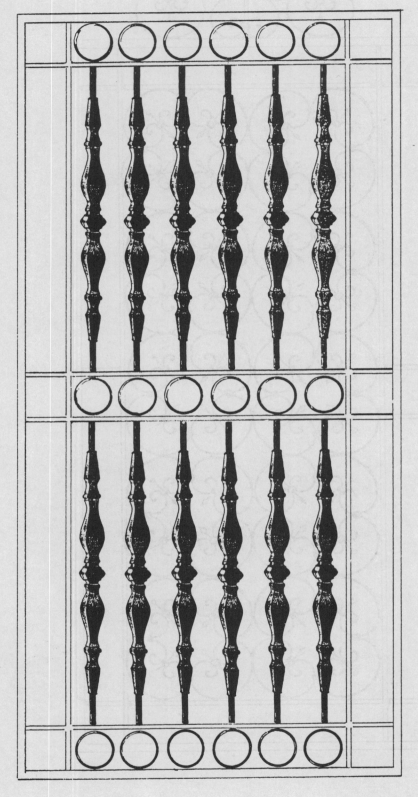

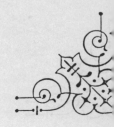

Art 144/1
Art 157/6

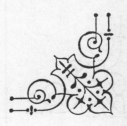

Art 55/2
Art 73/2
Art 119/21

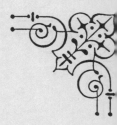
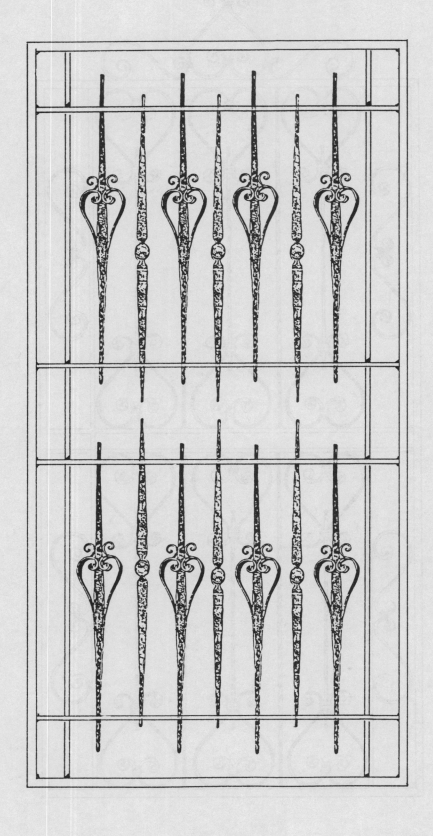

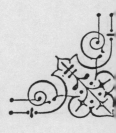

Art 96/2
Art 96/3

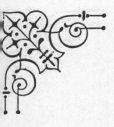

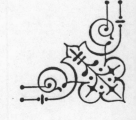

Art 19/5
Art 81/3

Art 22/2

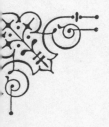
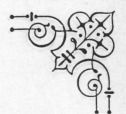

Art 33/1
Art 87/6

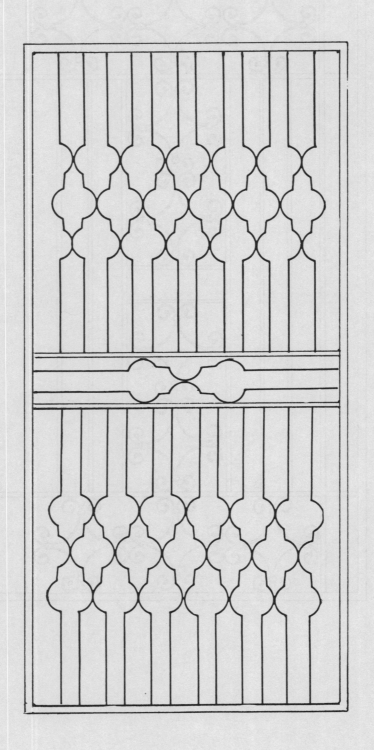

Art 142/8

25

Art 51/2   Art 88/10
Art 33/2   Art 119/23
Art 88/9

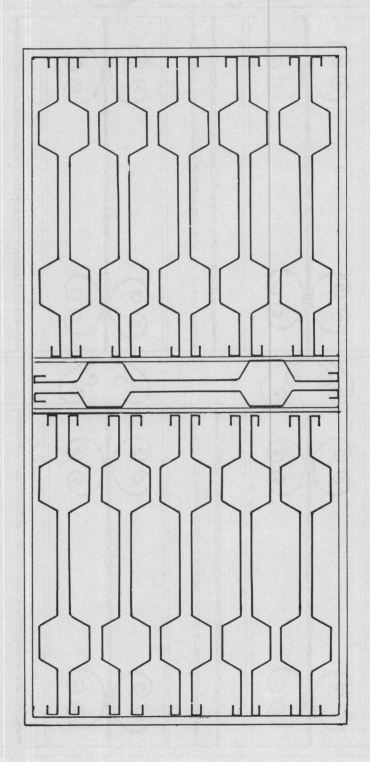

Art 142/6

Art 66/5
Art 74/3
Art 119/4

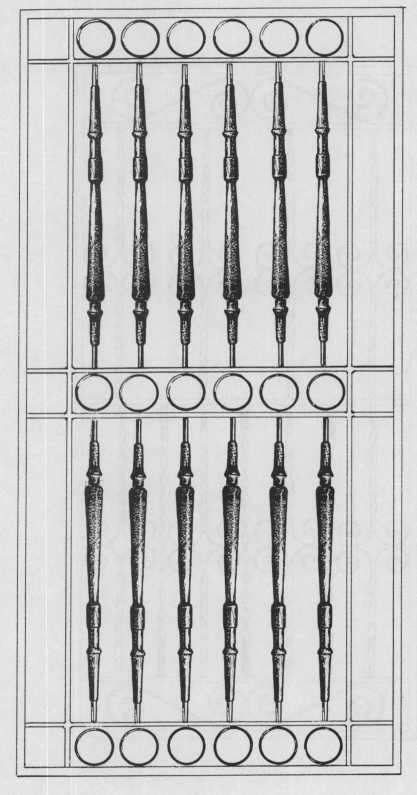

Art 145/1
Art 157/6

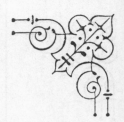
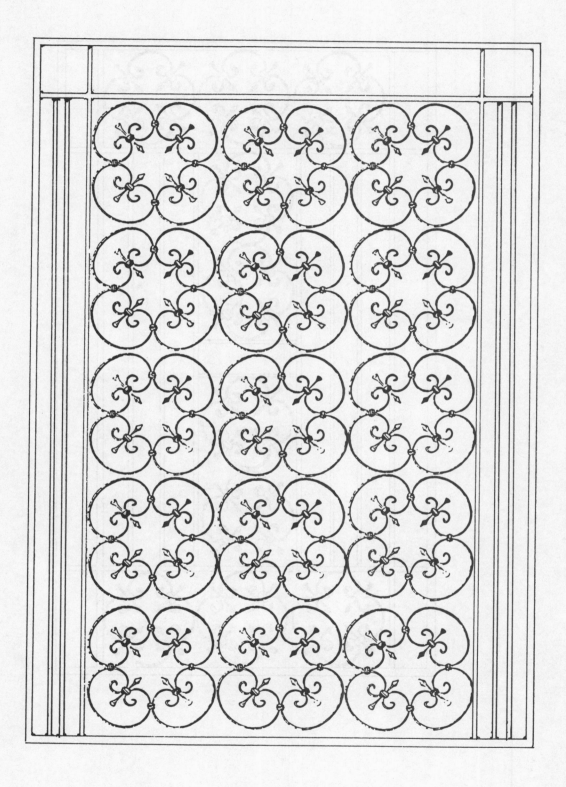

Art 24/2
(Art 24/1)

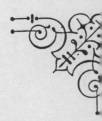

Art 17/1

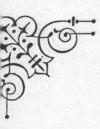

Art 24/1

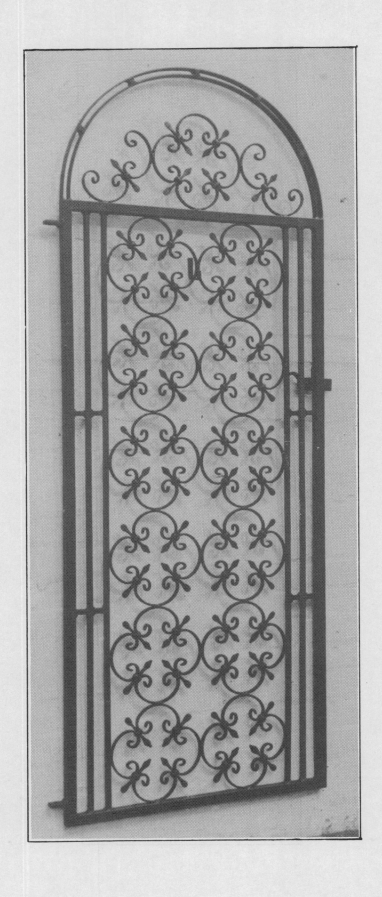

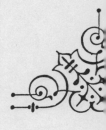

Art 23/1

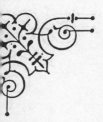

Art 54/6   Art 74/4
Art 74/22 Art 119/23

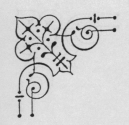

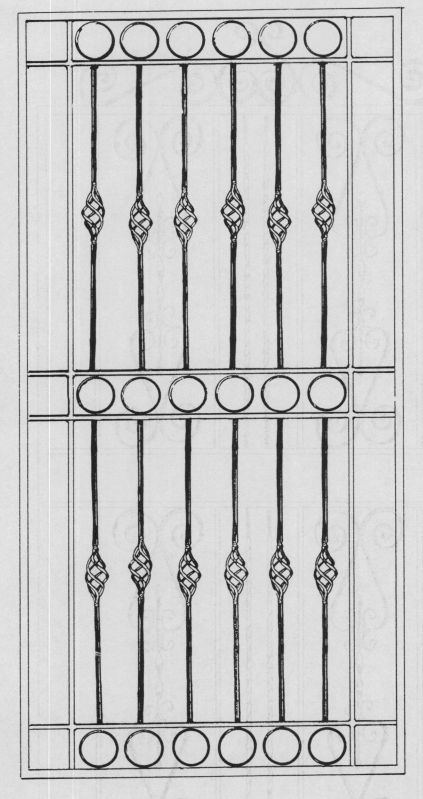

Art 66/1
Art 157/6

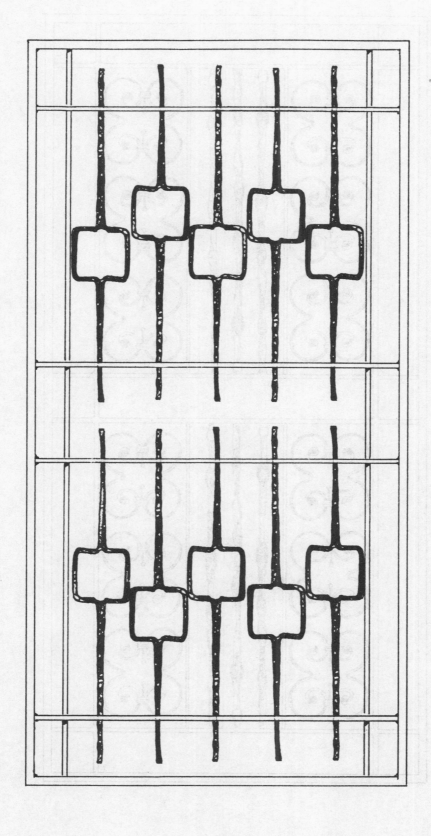

Art 104/1

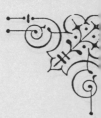

Art 29/1
Art 96/4

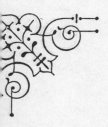

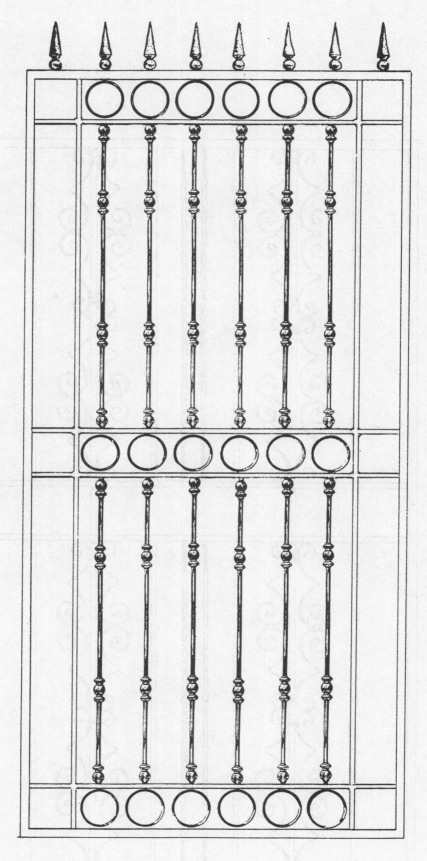

Art 151/6
Art 157/6
Art 121/4

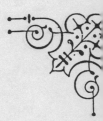

Art 35/1
Art 119/23

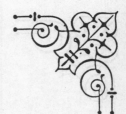

Art 19/3

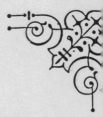

Art 141/2

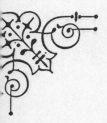

Art 49/3
Art 119/23
Art 124/8

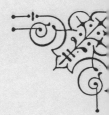

Art 67/3
Art 74/3
Art 119/4

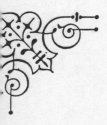
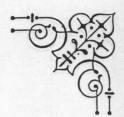

Art 33/2
Art 88/9
Art 88/10

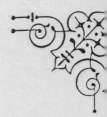
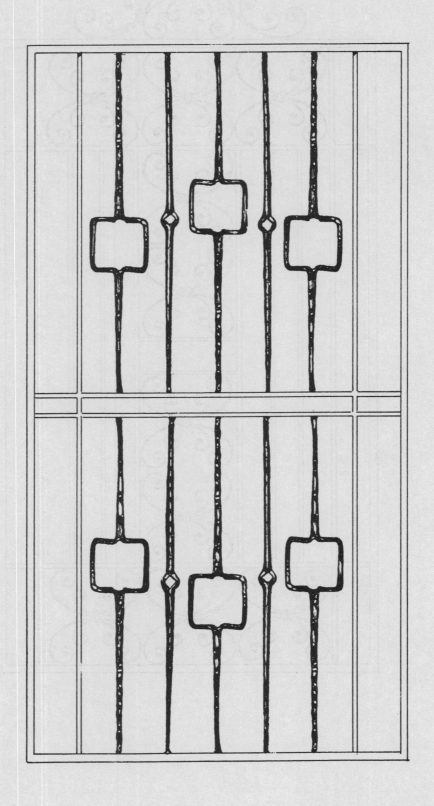

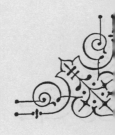

Art 104/1
Art 101/1

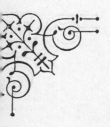
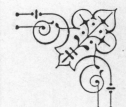

Art 96/1
Art 73/1
Art 73/2

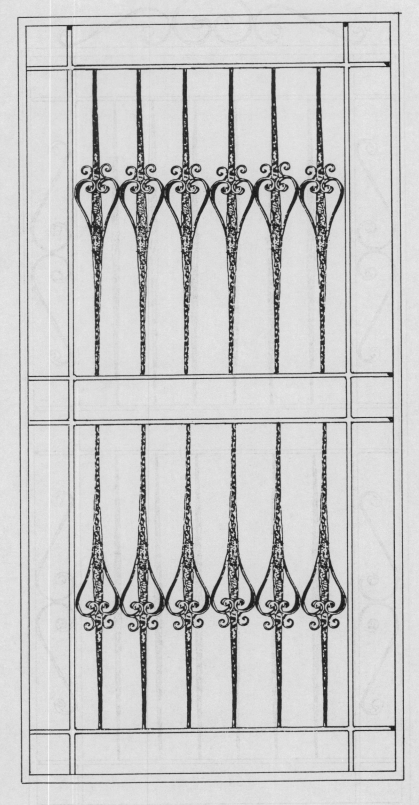

Art 96/3

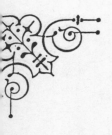
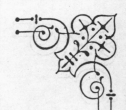
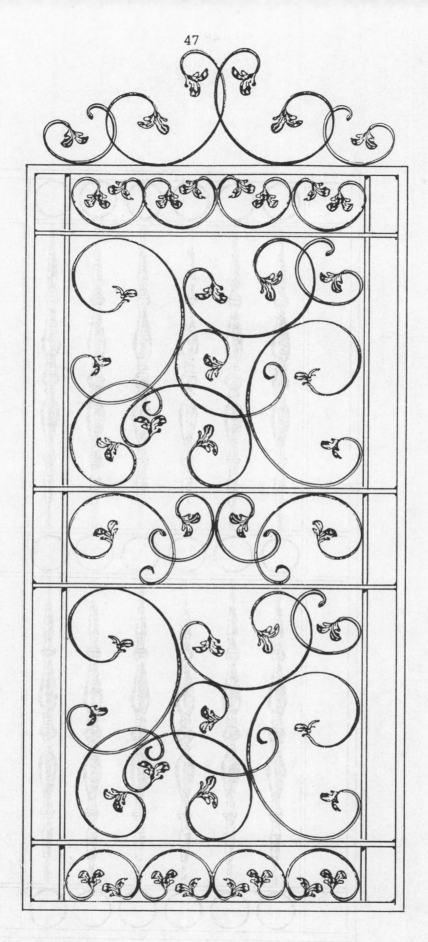

Art 93/1
Art 93/4
Art 94/1
Art 94/3   Art 94/2

48

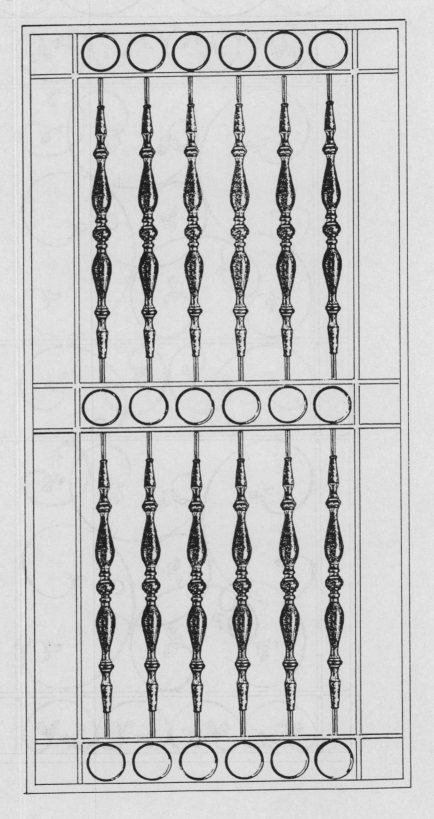

Art 145/2
Art 157/6

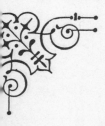

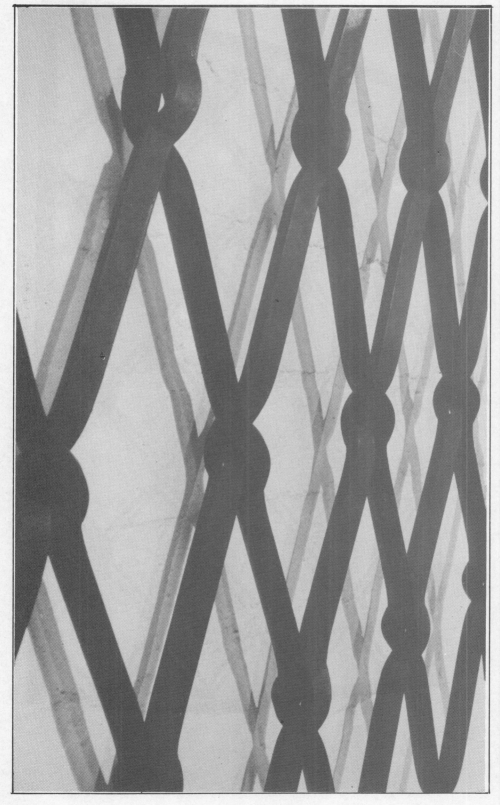

Art 40/1

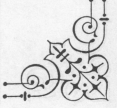

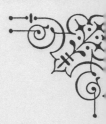

Art 39/1-2
Art 39/3

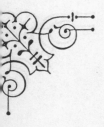

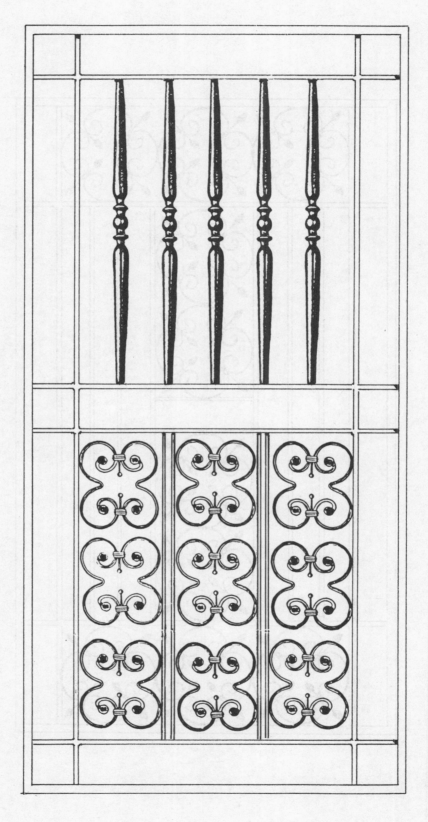

Art 29/1
Art 146/1

Art 23/2

Art 51/1
Art 33/2
Art 119/23

Art 96/2
Art 73/1

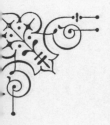

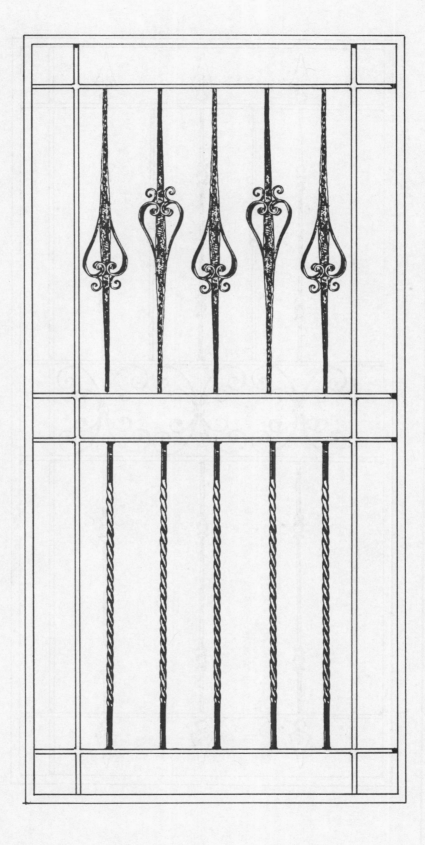

Art 96/3
Art 119/23

Art 155/2
Art 33/2
Art 125/2

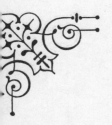

Art 119/14
Art 57/2
Art 83/1

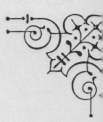

Art 33/2

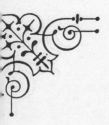

Art 54/6

Art 62/2

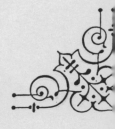

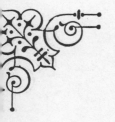

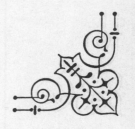

Art 23/2
Art 82/7

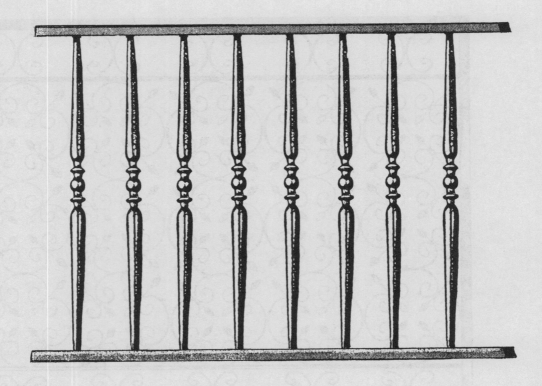

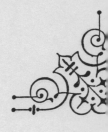

Art 146/1

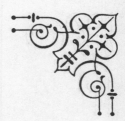
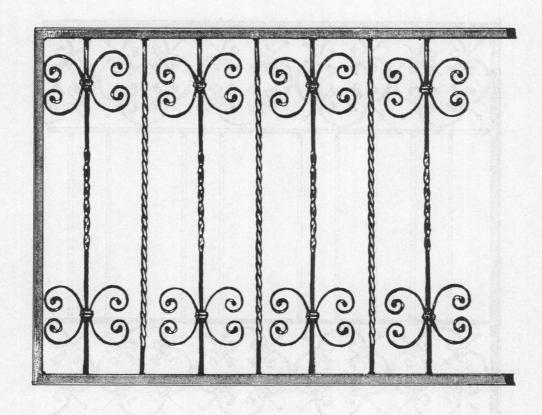

Art 51/2
Art 119/23

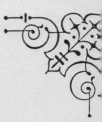

Art 19/3

Art 119/14
Art 19/5
Art 81/3

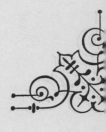

Art 35/1

Art 60/3

Art 29/1

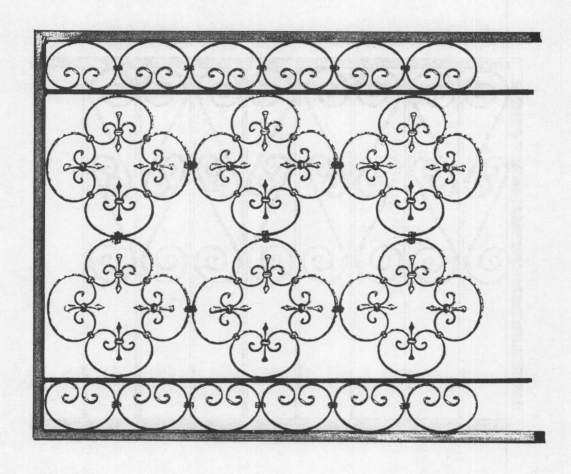

Art 24/1
Art 85/4

Art 75/33

Art 67/3 (67/4)
Art 74/15
Art 119/4/11

72

Art 23/1

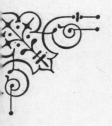

Art 66/1
(102/1)
(159/1-9)

Art 59/1

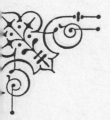

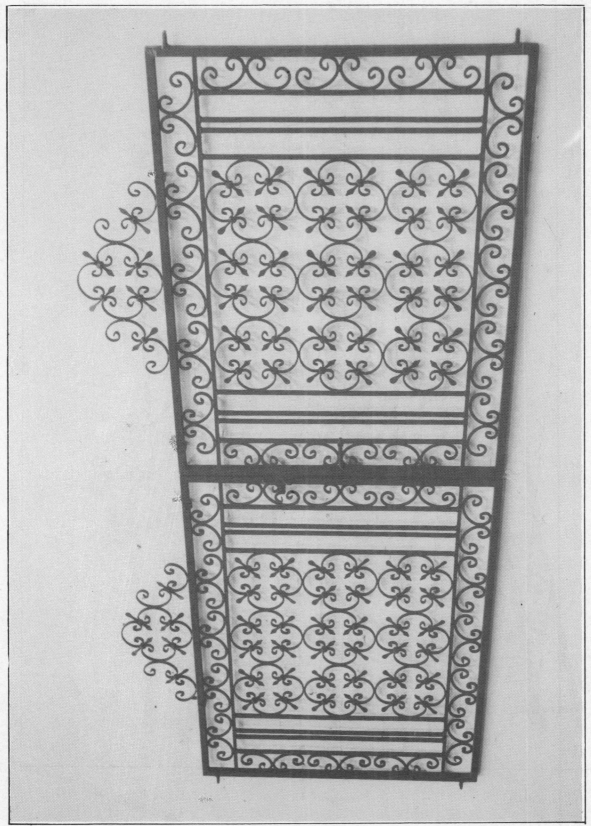

Art 23/1
Art 82/1

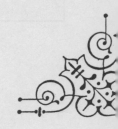

Art 70/1
Art 84/6
Art 119/4

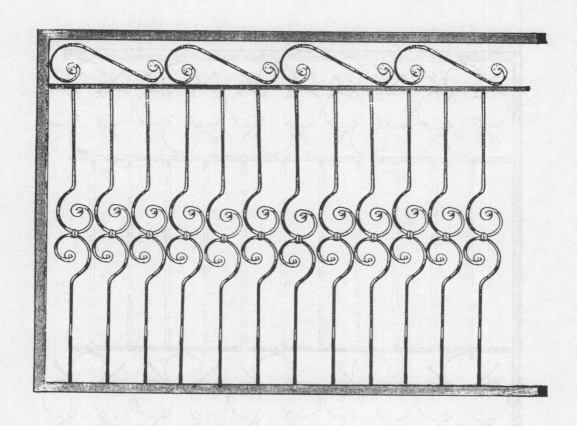

Art 57/4
Art 73/1

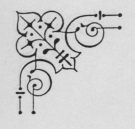

Art 21/4

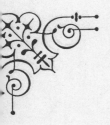

Art 58/3
Art 73/2

Art 64/2

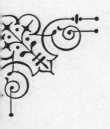
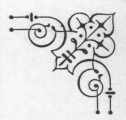

Art 35/1

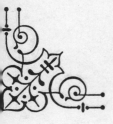

Art 17/1

Art 114/2
Art 52/2
Art 119/23

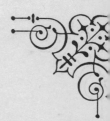

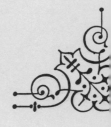

Art 68/2
Art 84/4

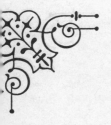

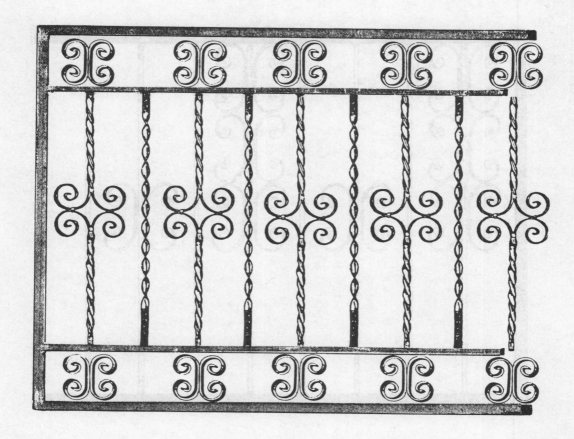

Art 66/5/6/7
Art 78/3
Art 119/4/11/18

Art 73/3

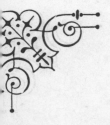

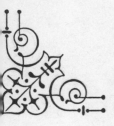

Art 76/4

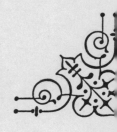

Art 19/5

Art 56/6

Art 70/1
Art 84/6

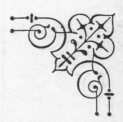

Art 70/1
Art 84/6
Art 77/1
Art 119/4

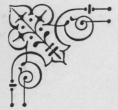

Art 51/3
Art 88/10

Art 51/3
Art 119/23

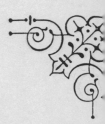

Art 17/1

Art 21/4
Art 119/21

96

Art 64/2
Art 157/9

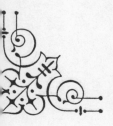

Art 60/3

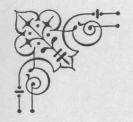

Art 84/4

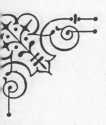

Art 20/3 Art (20/4)
Art 119/14

Art 20/4

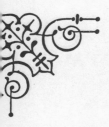

Art 38/1/2/3/4
Art 119/21

Art 37/2

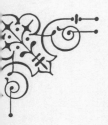

Art 51/3

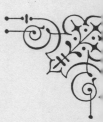
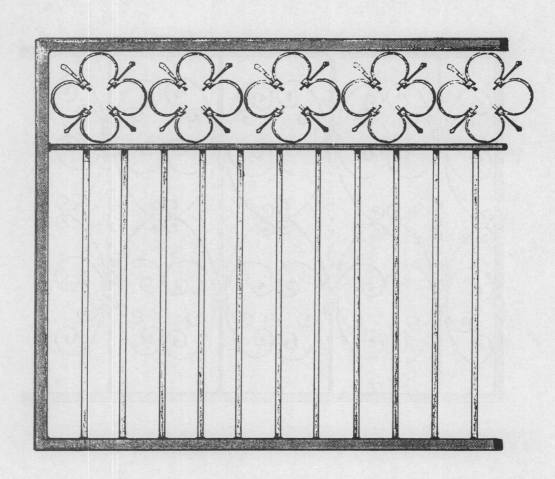

Art 21/4

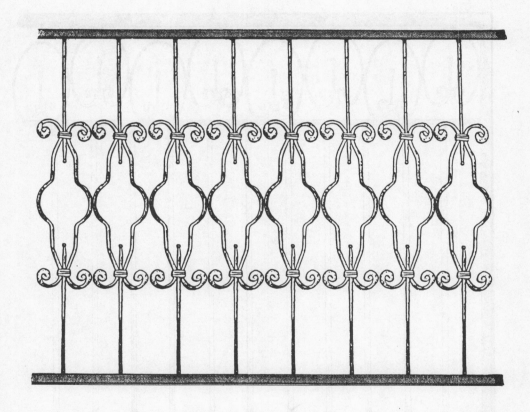

Art 56/6

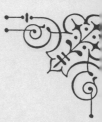

Art 92/1

Art 23/1
Art 82/1

Art 24/1
Art 82/1
Art 90/2

Art 17/1
Art 81/7

Art 84/4

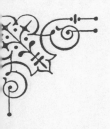

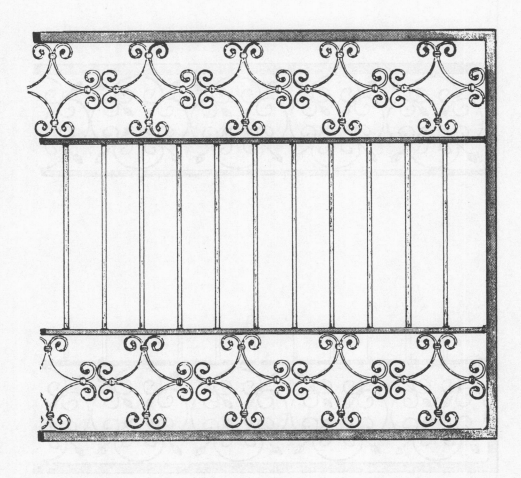

Art 33/1

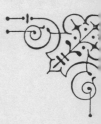

Art 23/2

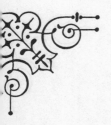
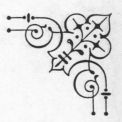

Art 51/2
Art 51/1

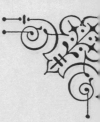

Art 66/3 (159/1-9)

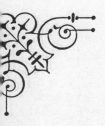

Art 119/14
Art 57/1
Art 73/1

Art 33/3

Art 60/3

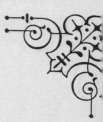

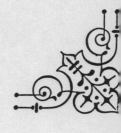

Art 84/3

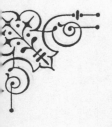

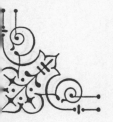

Art 23/1
Art 82/1

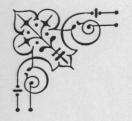

Art 22/2

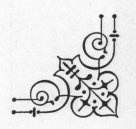

Art 37/2

Art 16/1

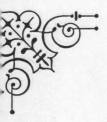

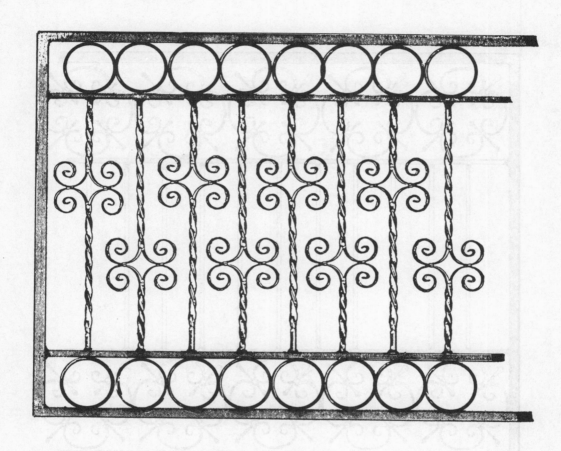

Art 66/8
Art 157/8

Art 18/2

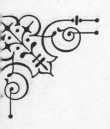

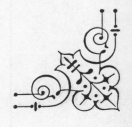

Art 49/3

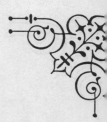

Art 84/4

Art 58/3
Art 73/1

Art 23/2

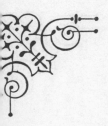

Art 114/2
Art 52/2

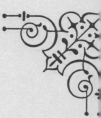

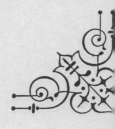

Art 83/1

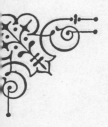

Art 17/1
Art 81/7
Art 119/21

Art 75/33

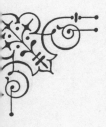

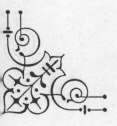

Art 51/3

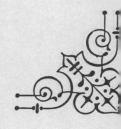

Art 19/3

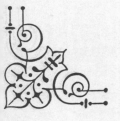

Art 57/4
Art 73/2
Art 119/14

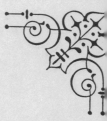

136

Art 84/6

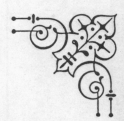

Art 73/2

Art 76/4

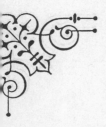

Art 35/1

Art 23/1

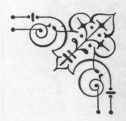

Art 85/4

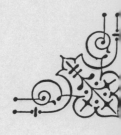

Art 84/3

Art 18/2
Art 119/14

Art 18/2

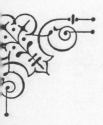

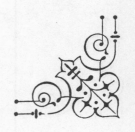

Art 151/1
Art 157/6

Art 24/1
Art 82/1

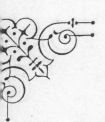
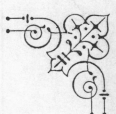
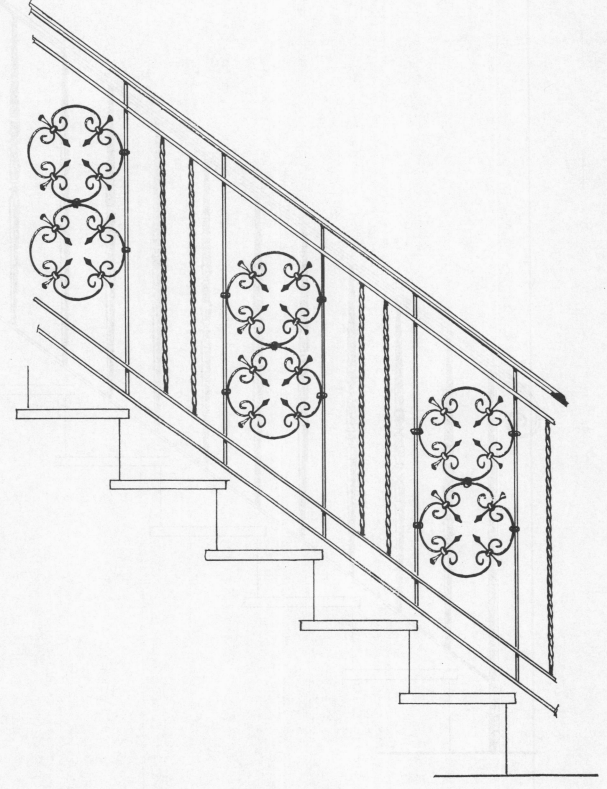

Art 114/2
Art 23/1
Art 119/14

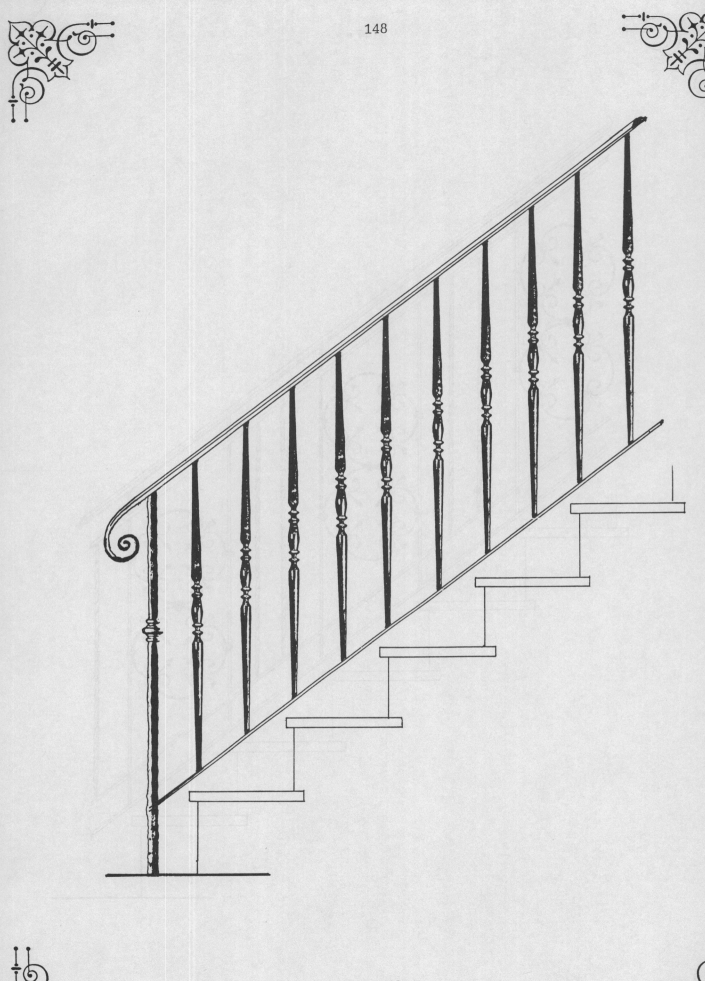

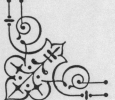

Art 149/1
Art 112/8
Art 114/2
Art 115/3

Art 54/2
Art 119/23
Art 112/7
Art 114/2
Art 115/2

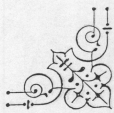

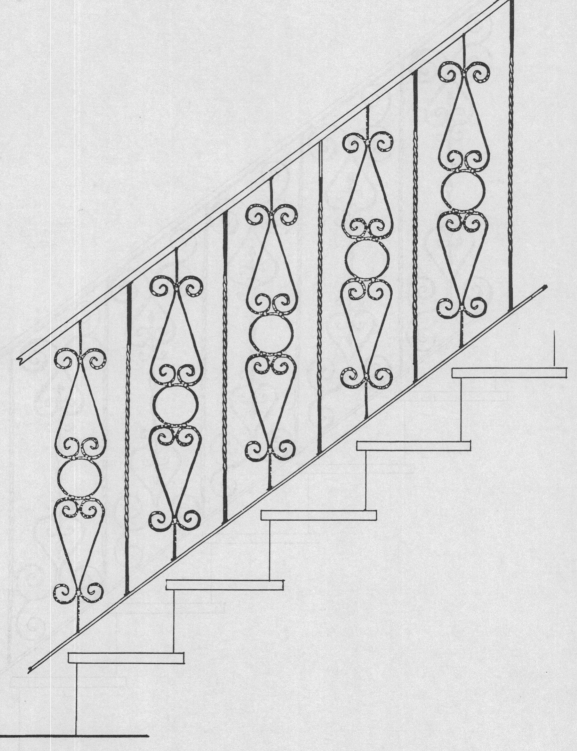

Art 114/2
Art 64/2
Art 119/21

Art 69/1
Art 119/18

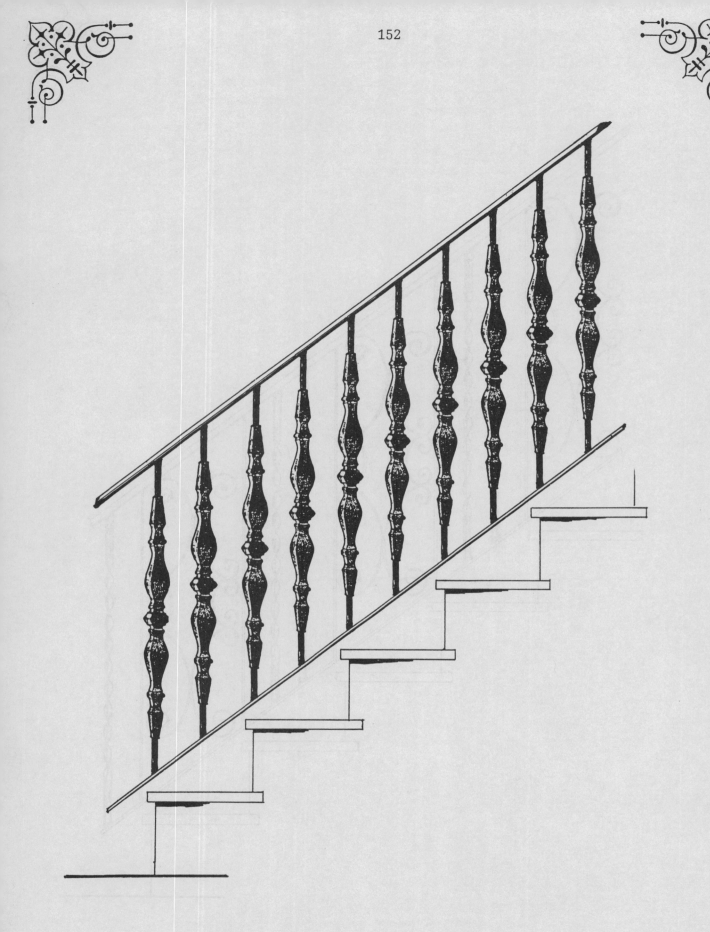

Art 114/2
Art 144/1

153

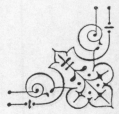

Art 62/2
Art 112/5/6
Art 114/2
Art 115/3

154

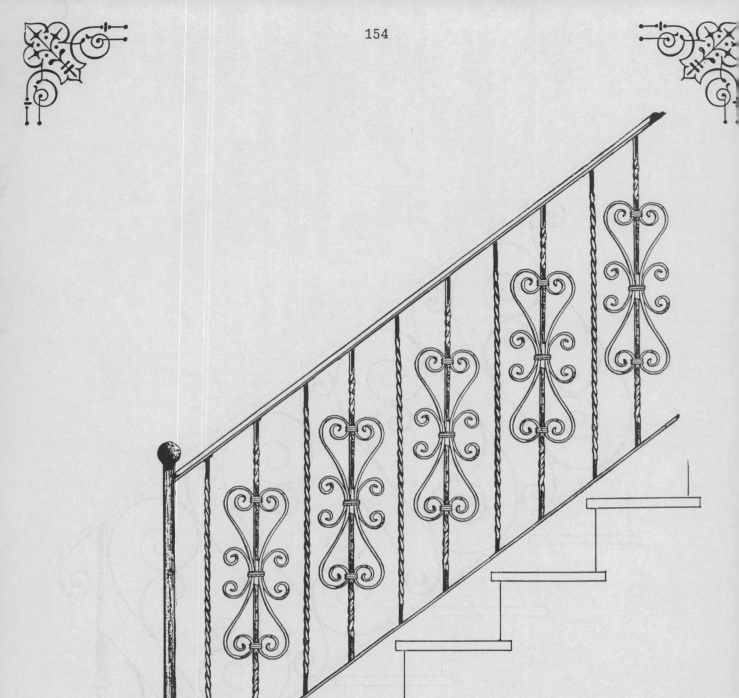

Art 49/3
Art 119/23
Art 114/2
Art 117/7

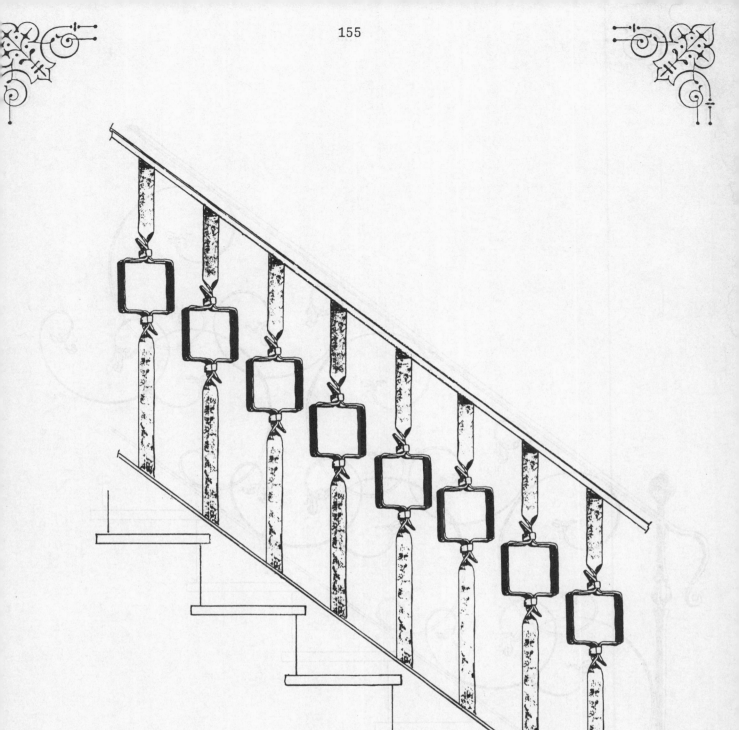

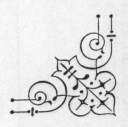

Art 61/1-4

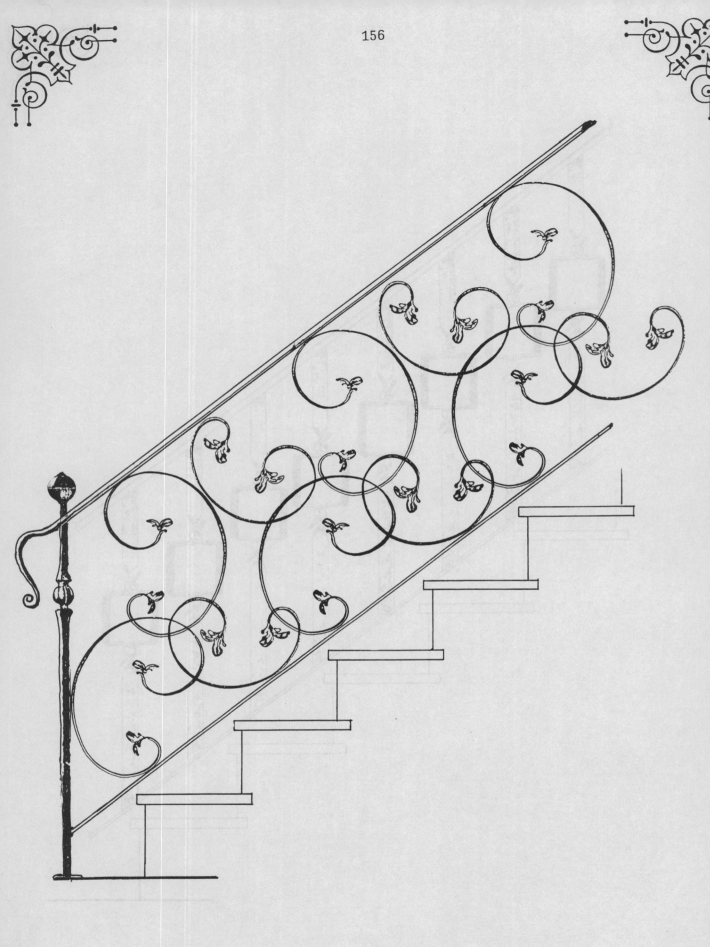

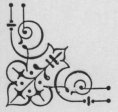

Art 93/1   Art 113/9
Art 93/4   Art 114/2
Art 112/8   Art 115/2

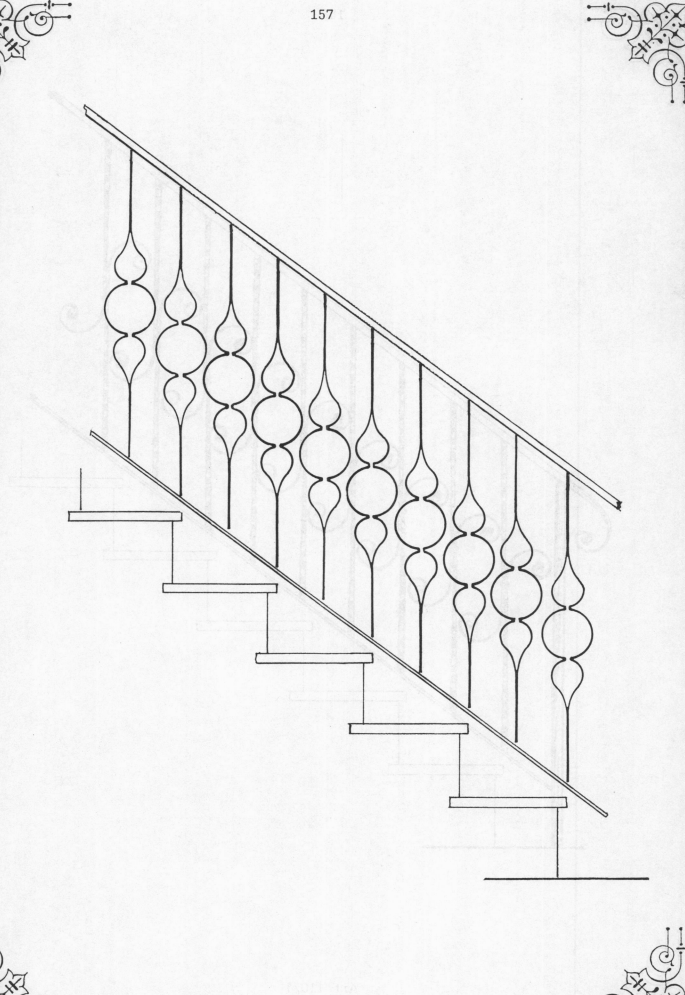

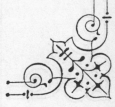

Art 141/ 1

158

Art 110/1
Art 114/2
Art 115/3

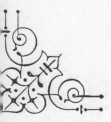

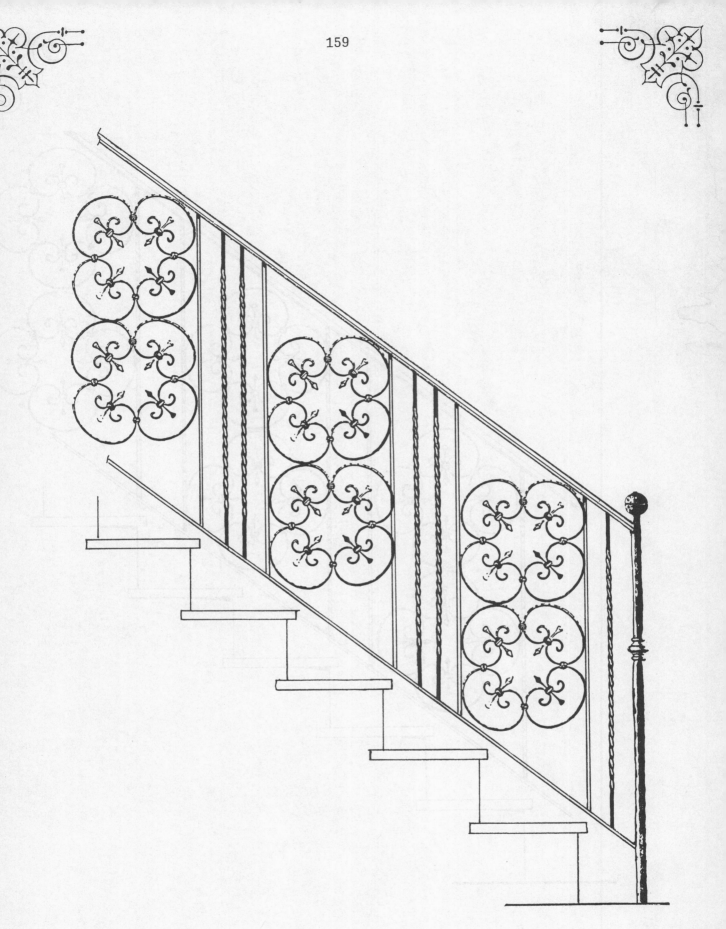

Art 24/1 (24/2)
Art 119/23
Art 113/10
Art 112/5 (112/6)
Art 114/2

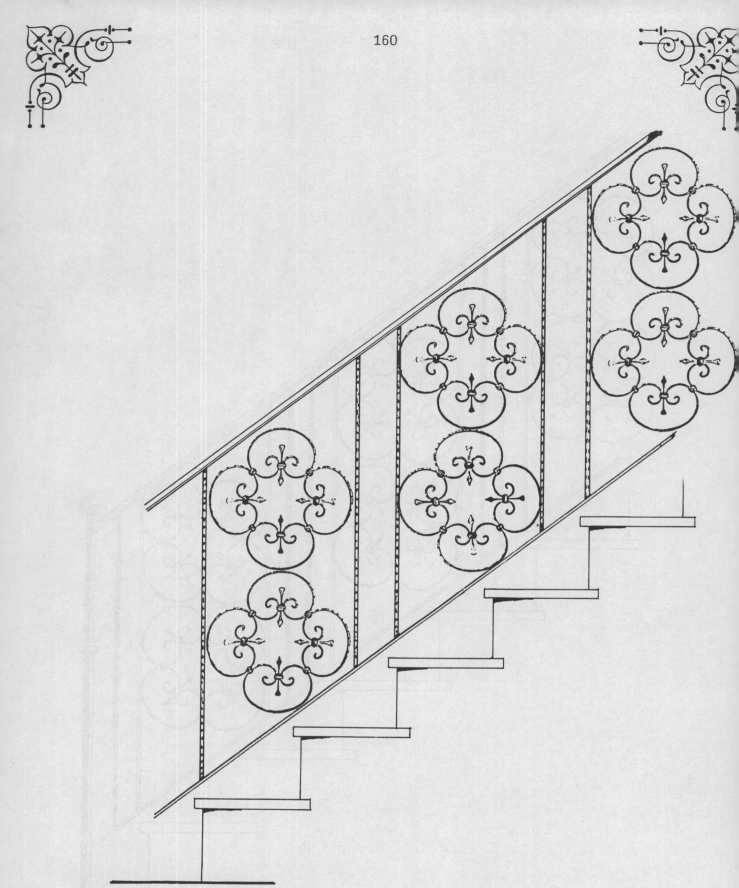

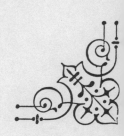

Art 24/1 (24/2)
Art 118/1
Art 114/5

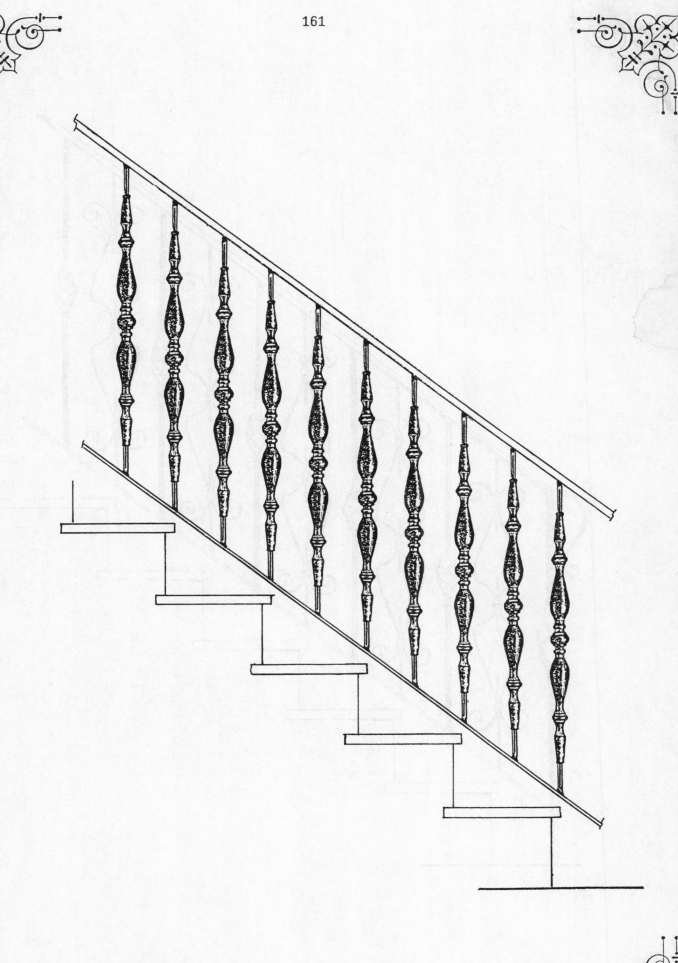

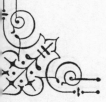

Art 145/2

162

Art 66/1
Art 59/1
Art 112/2
Art 114/2
Art 115/2

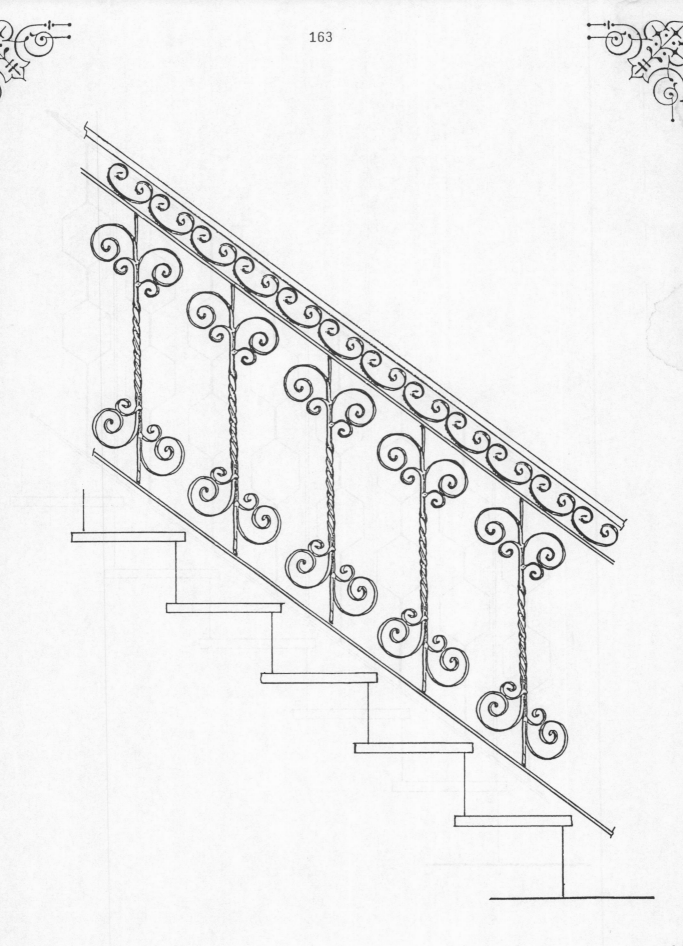

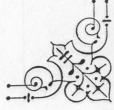

Art 67/1-2
Art 84/6

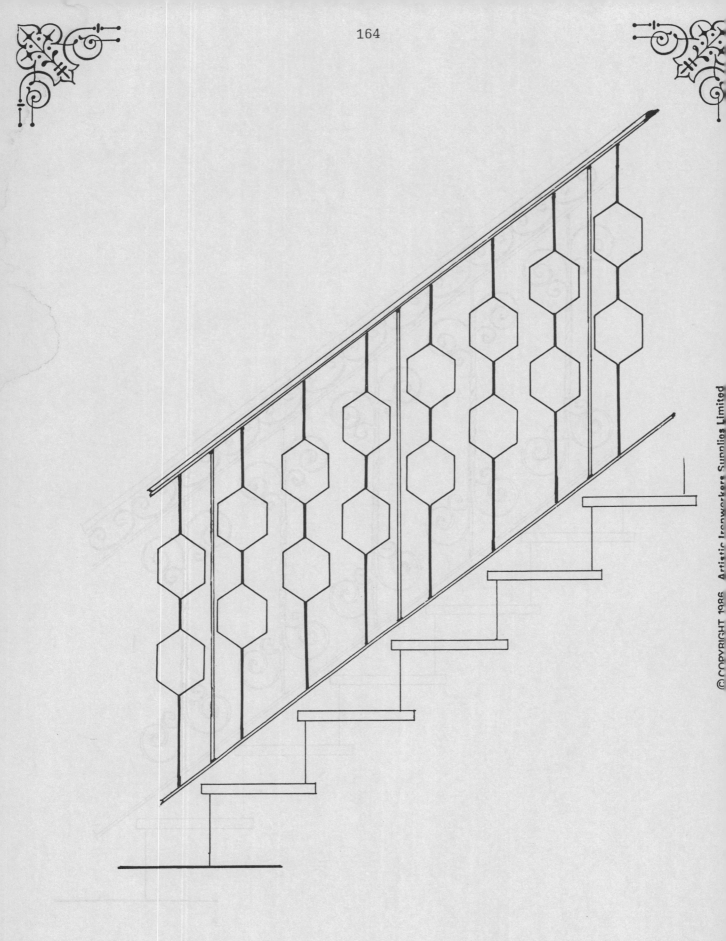

Art **114**/2
Art 141/2

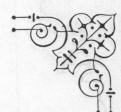

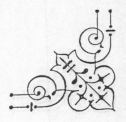

Art 29/1
Art 83/1
Art 112/3-4
Art 113/11
Art 114/2

Art 114/2
Art 51/1
Art 119/23

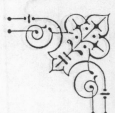

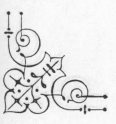

Art 55/5-6
Art 73/2
Art 119/21   Art 114/2

Art 37/2
Art 118/1
Art 114/2

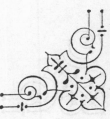

Art 52/2
Art 112/3-4
Art 113/11
Art 115/2   Art 114/2

170

Art 35/1
Art 66/1
Art 119/23   Art 117/9
Art 112/6   Art 114/2

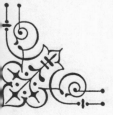

Art 57/2
Art 119/21
Art 112/8
Art 114/2   Art 117/9

172

Art 114/2
Art 68/2

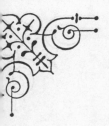
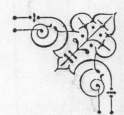
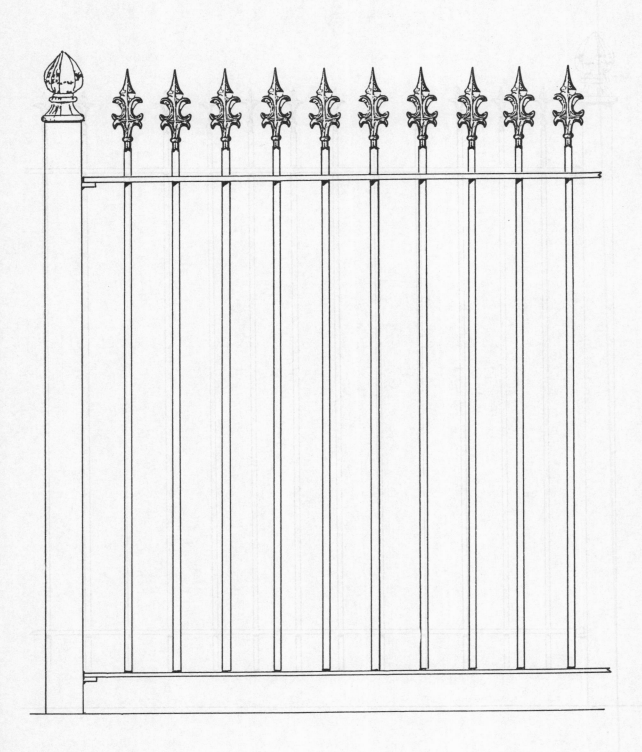

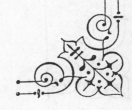

Art 124/8
Art 128/31

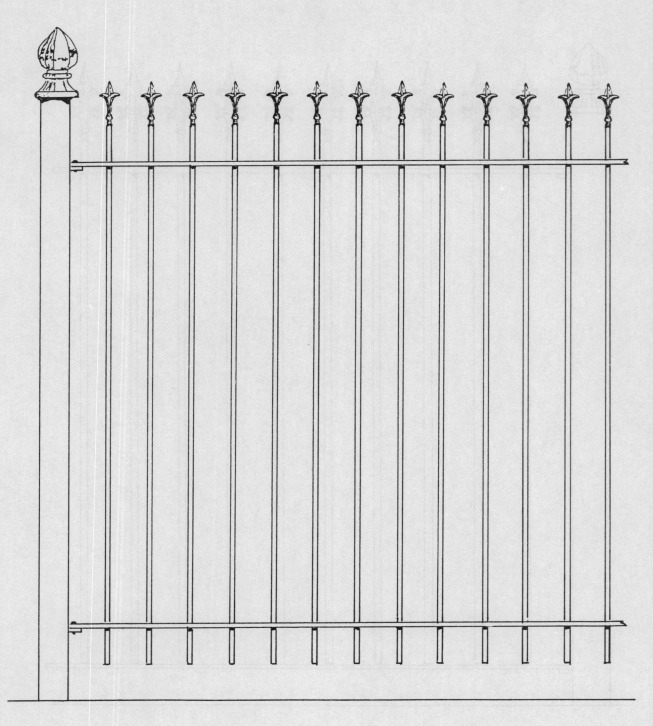

Art 124/3
Art 128/31

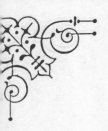

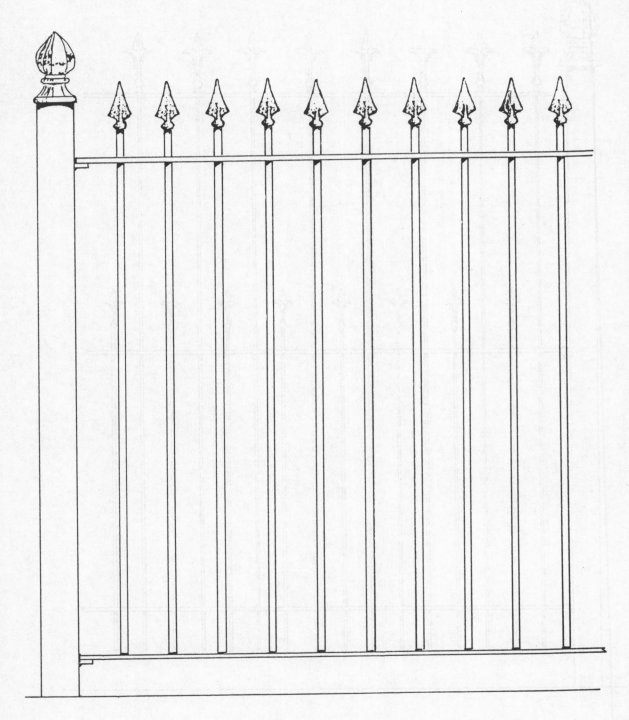
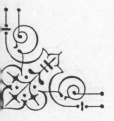

Art 125/1
Art 128/31

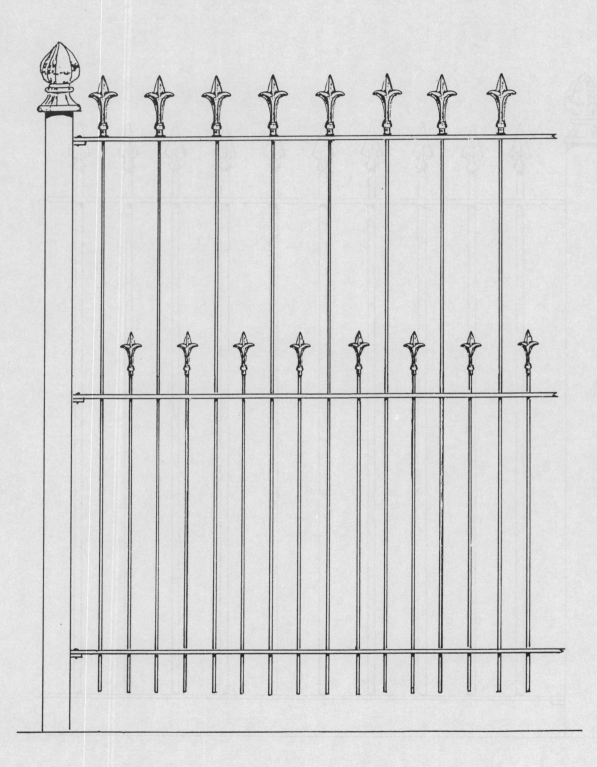

Art 124/4
Art 124/3
Art 128/31

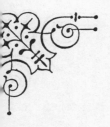
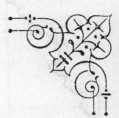

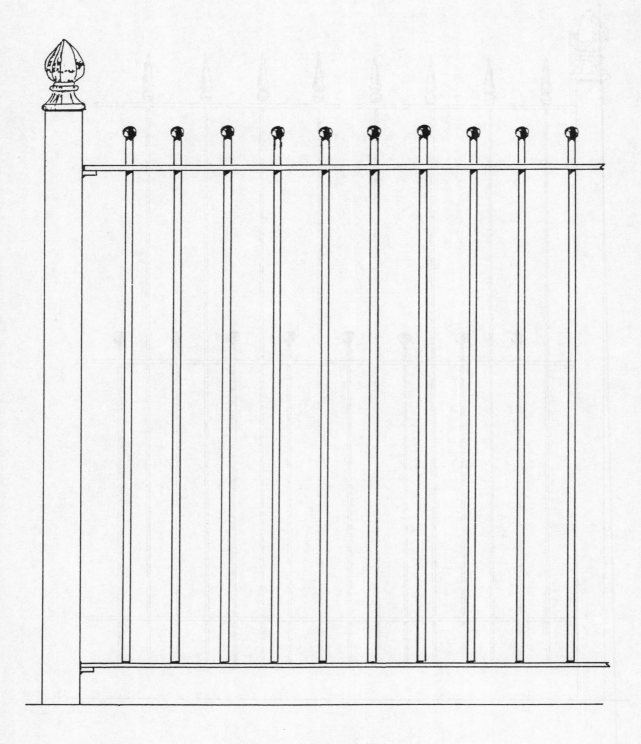

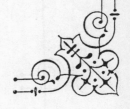

Art 117/5
Art 128/31

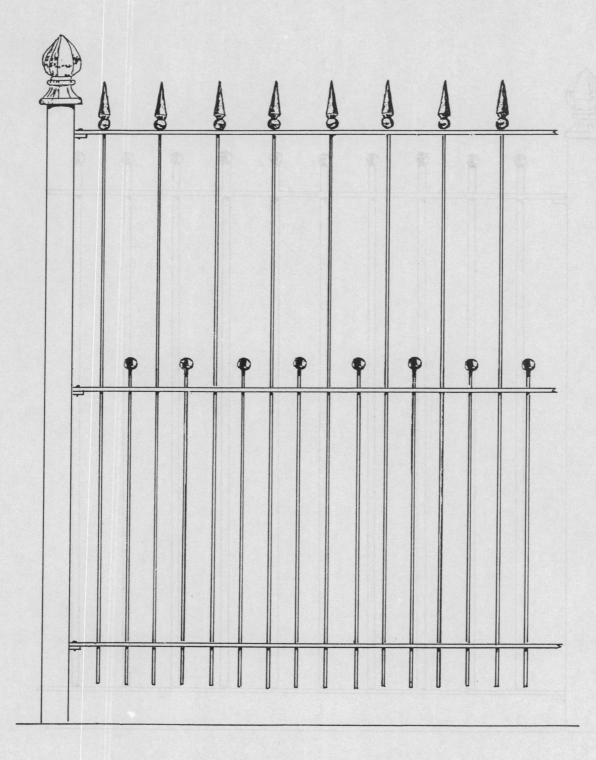

Art 121/4 (123/3)
Art 117/4
Art 128/31

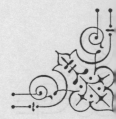

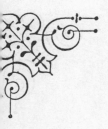
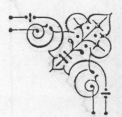
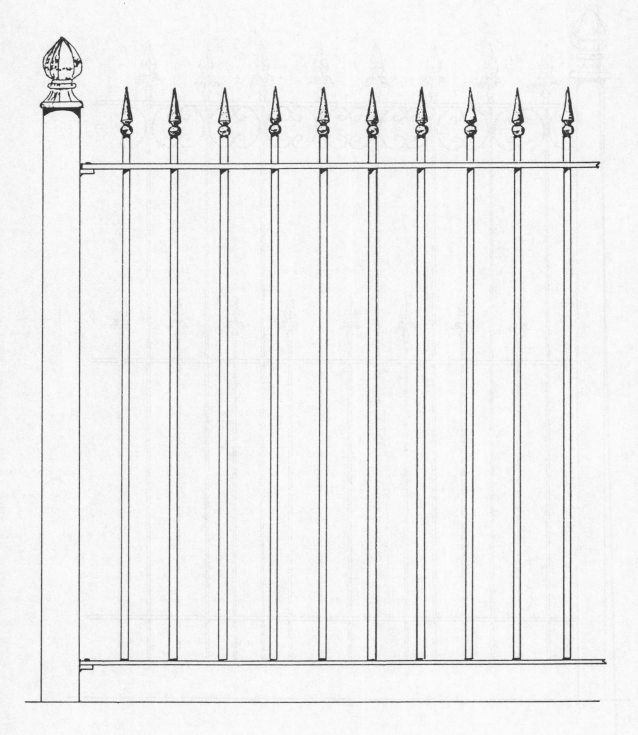

Art 121/4
Art 128/31

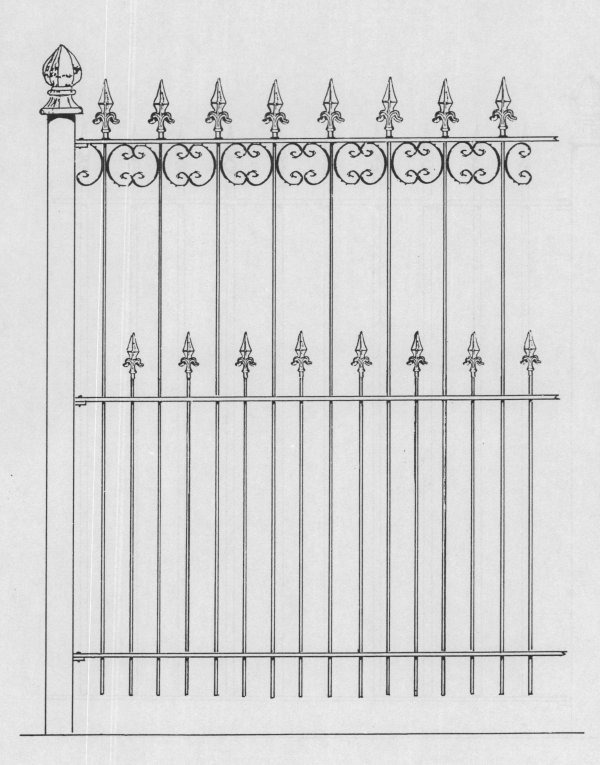

Art 124/1
Art 124/2
Art 82/1
Art 128/31

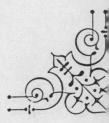

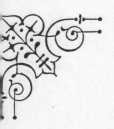

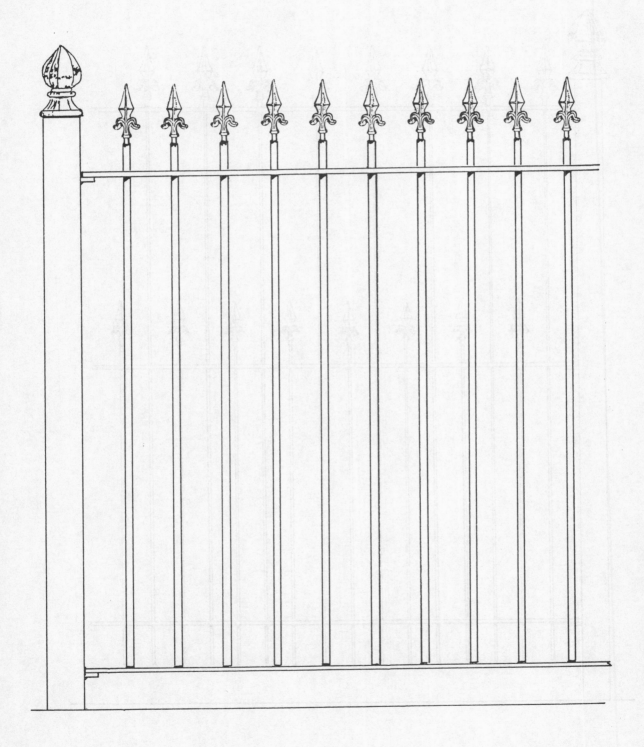

Art 124/2
Art 128/31

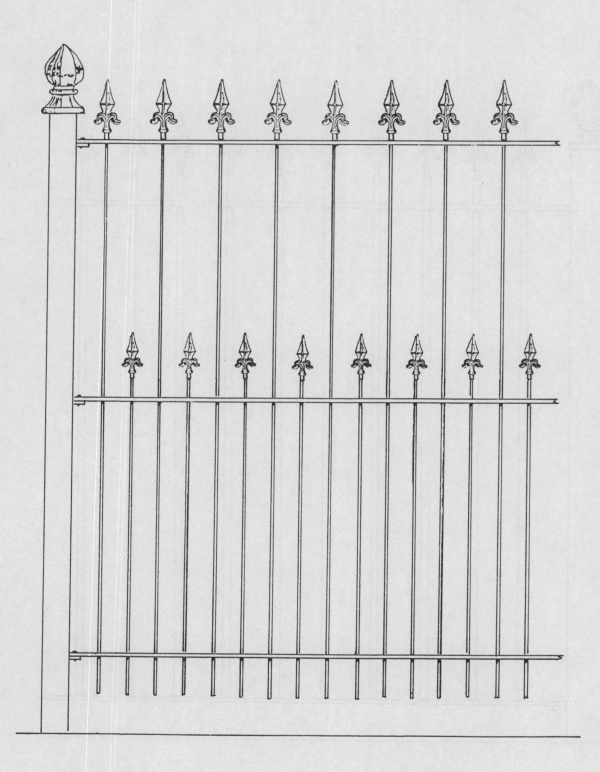

Art 124/1
Art 124/2
Art 128/31

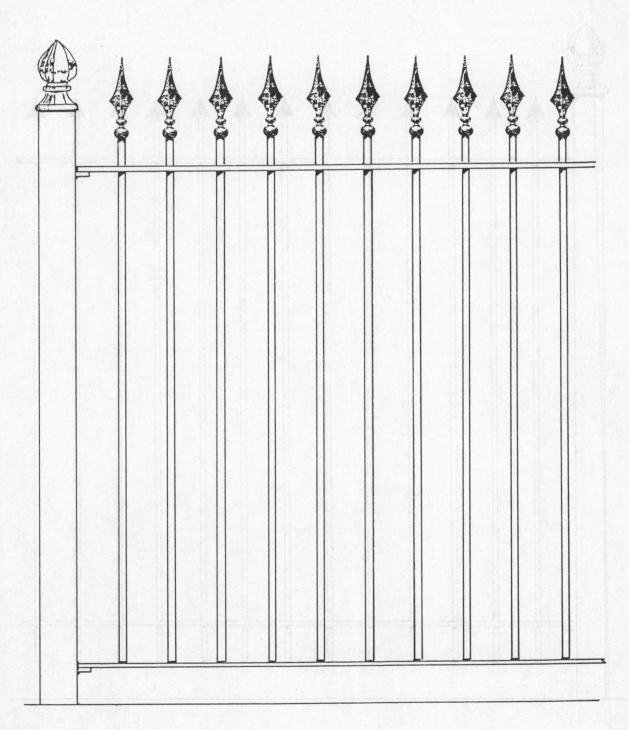

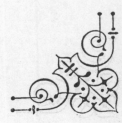

Art 120/1
Art 128/31

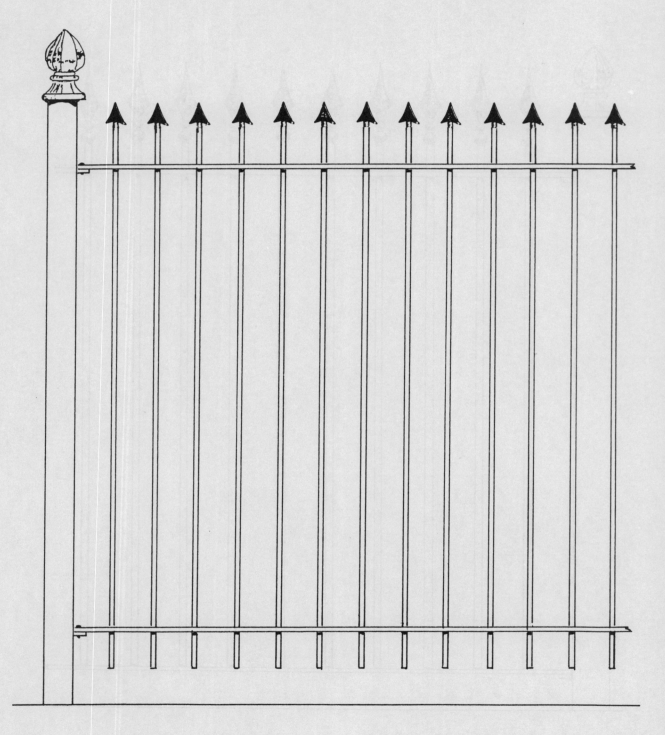

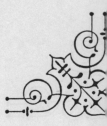

Art 127/2
Art 128/31

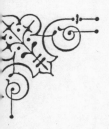

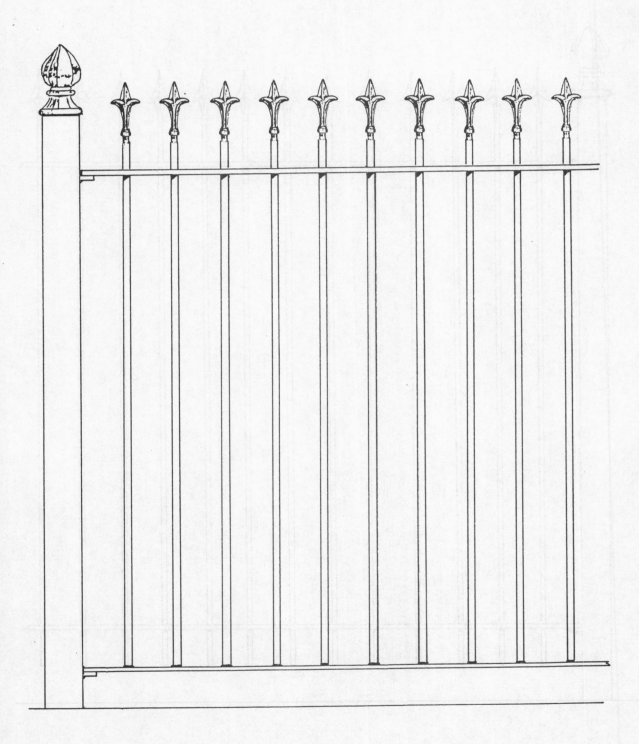
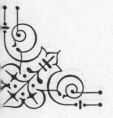

Art 124/4
Art 128/31

Art 124/6
Art 128/31

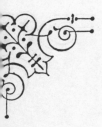

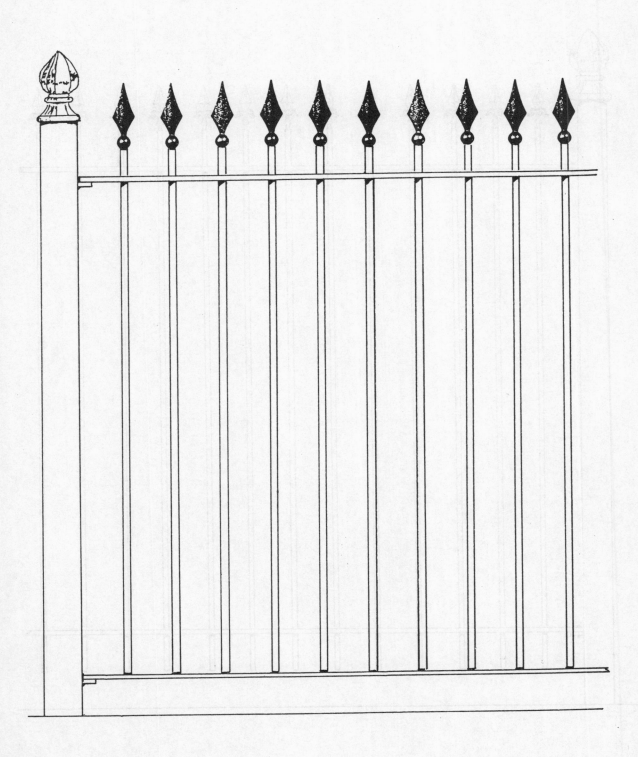

Art 123/6 (121/3)
Art 128/31

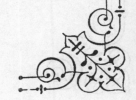

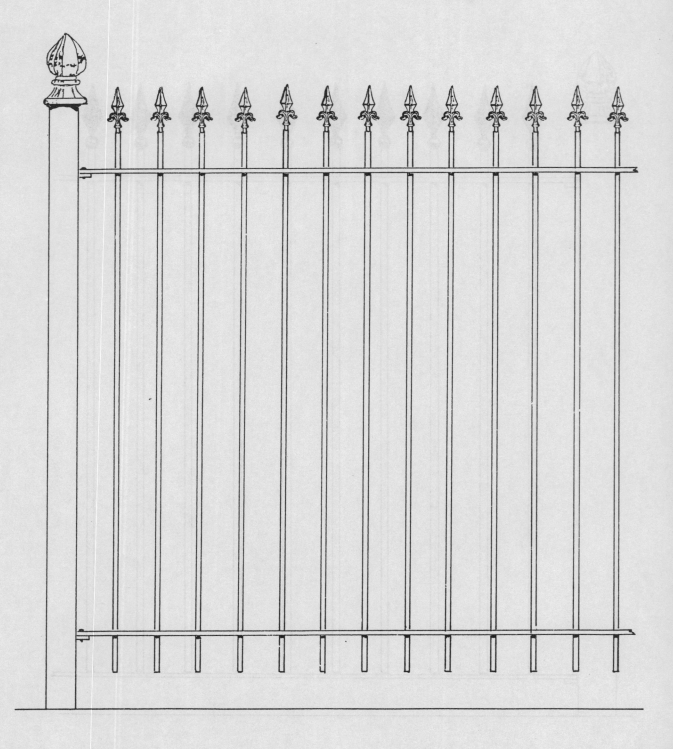

Art 124/1
Art 128/31

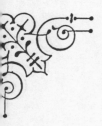

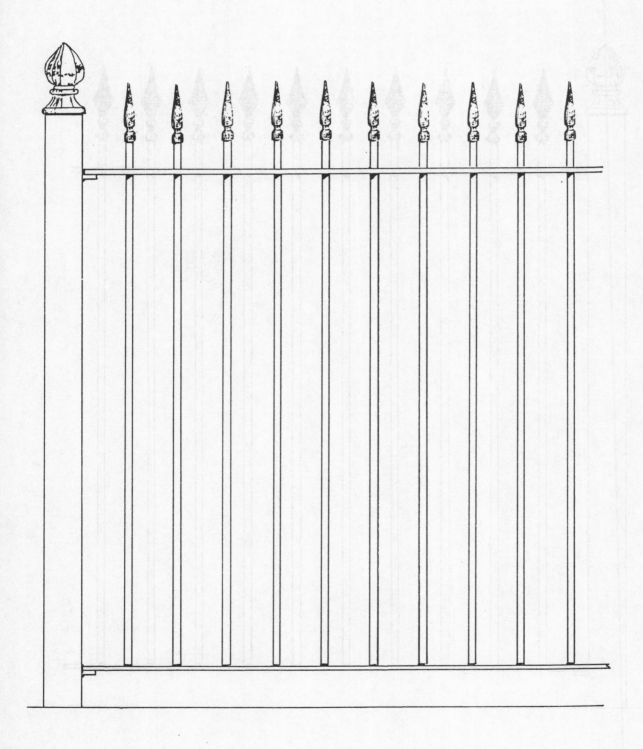

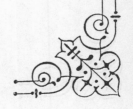

Art 123/5 (121/5)
Art 128/31

Art 123/7
Art 128/31

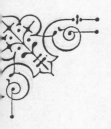

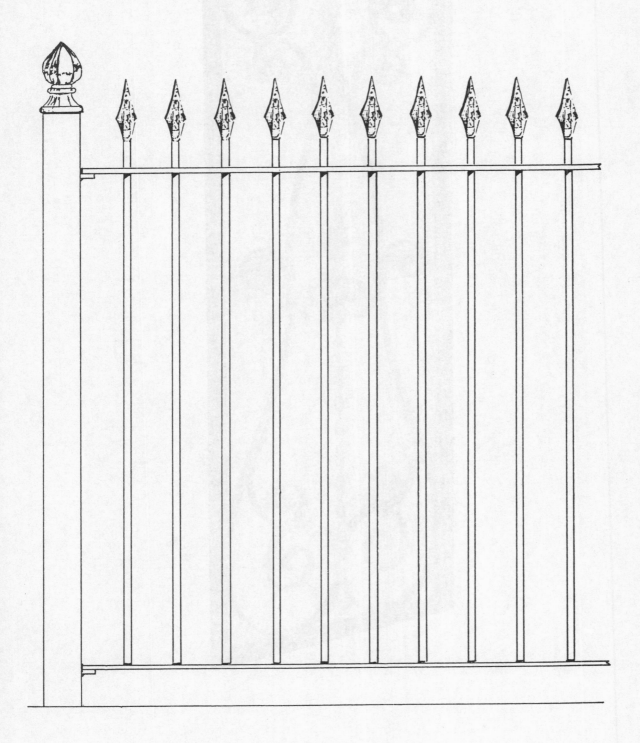

Art 122/1
Art 128/31

Art 62/2
Art 119/6
Art 121/3
Art 158/40

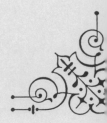

Art 72/1
Art 119/23
Art 120/1

Art 72/4
Art 156/6
Art 123/6

Art 24/2
Art 159/5
Art 125/1

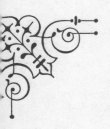

Art 34/1
Art 34/2
Art 119/16
Art 121/5 (123/5) Art 113/12

Art 60/3
Art 156/6
Art 72/4
Art 120/1

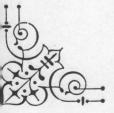

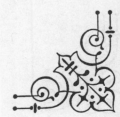

Art 63/4
Art 78/11
Art 157/6
Art 123/6

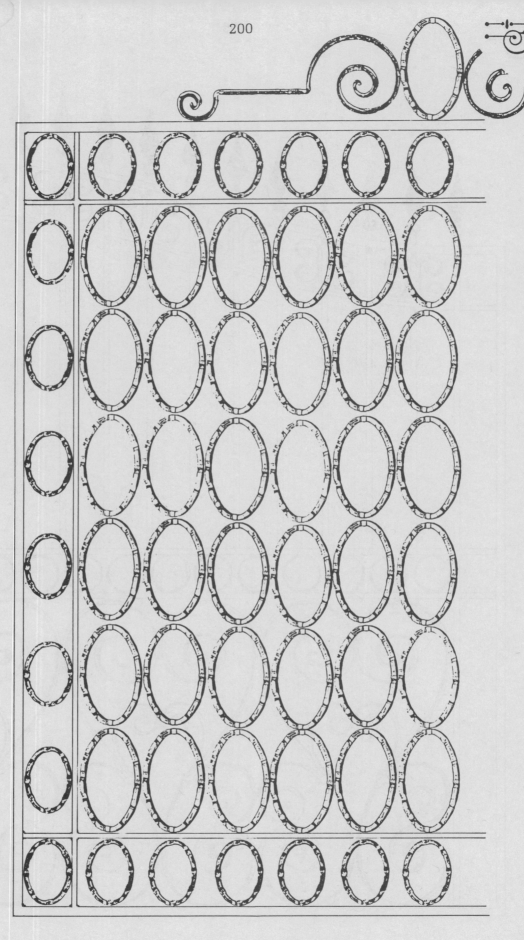

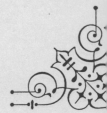

Art 156/6
Art 156/3
Art 72/4

201

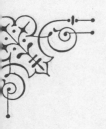
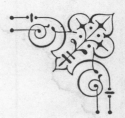
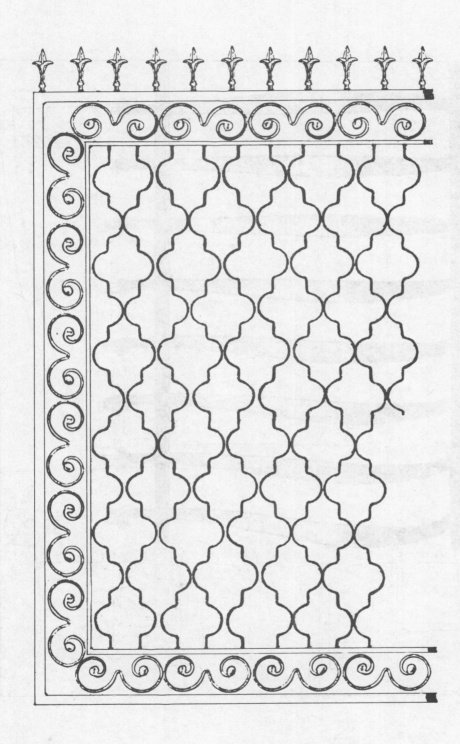

Art 38/(1-4)
Art 83/1
Art 124/3

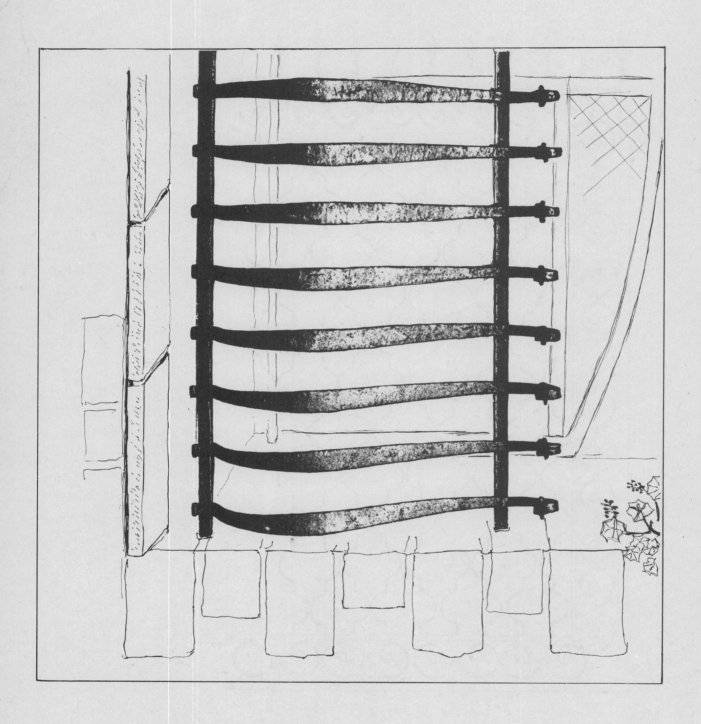

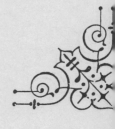

Art 110/2

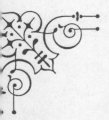

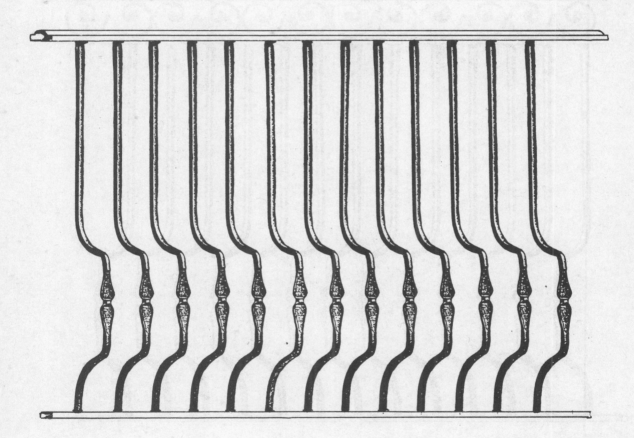

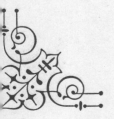

Art 134/30
Art 114/2

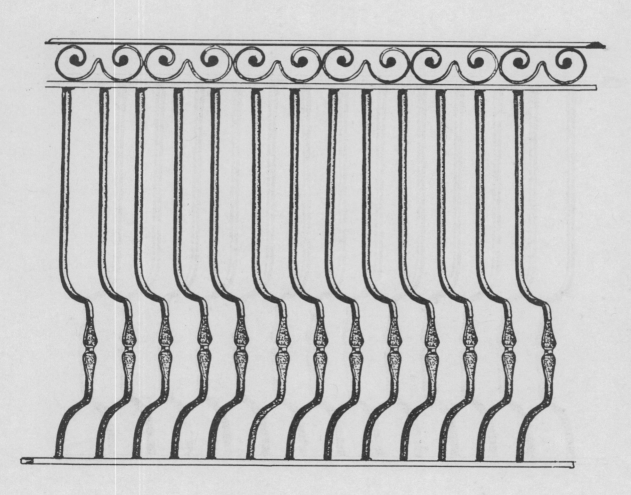

Art 134/30
Art 83/1
Art 114/2

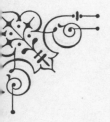

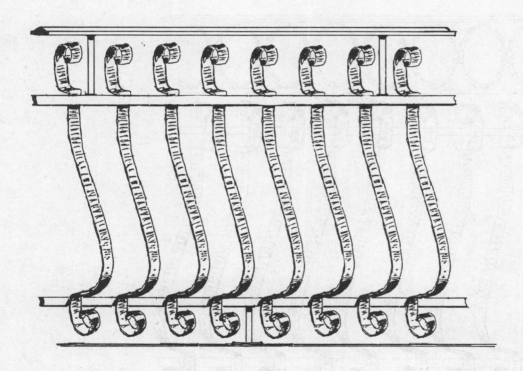

Art 46/4
Art 114/2

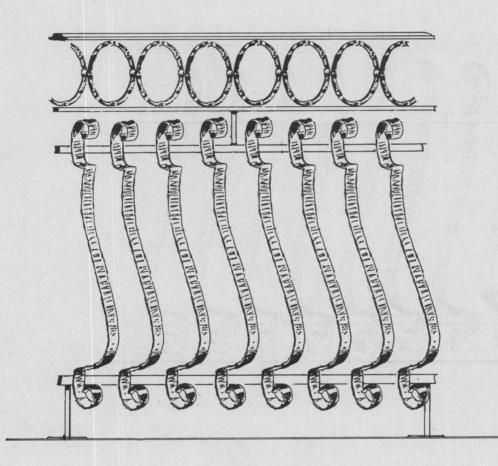

Art 46/4
Art 156/3

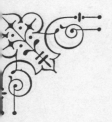

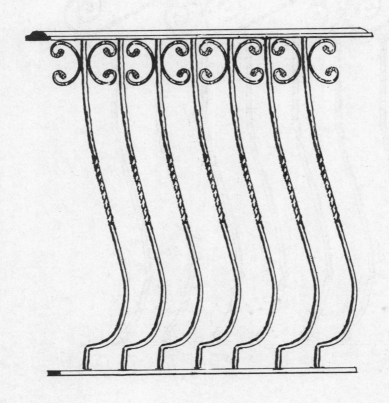

Art 47/3
Art 87/1
Art 114/2

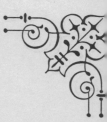

Art 142/4
Art 74/3

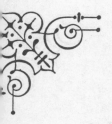

Art 142/4
Art 87/3
Art 119/21

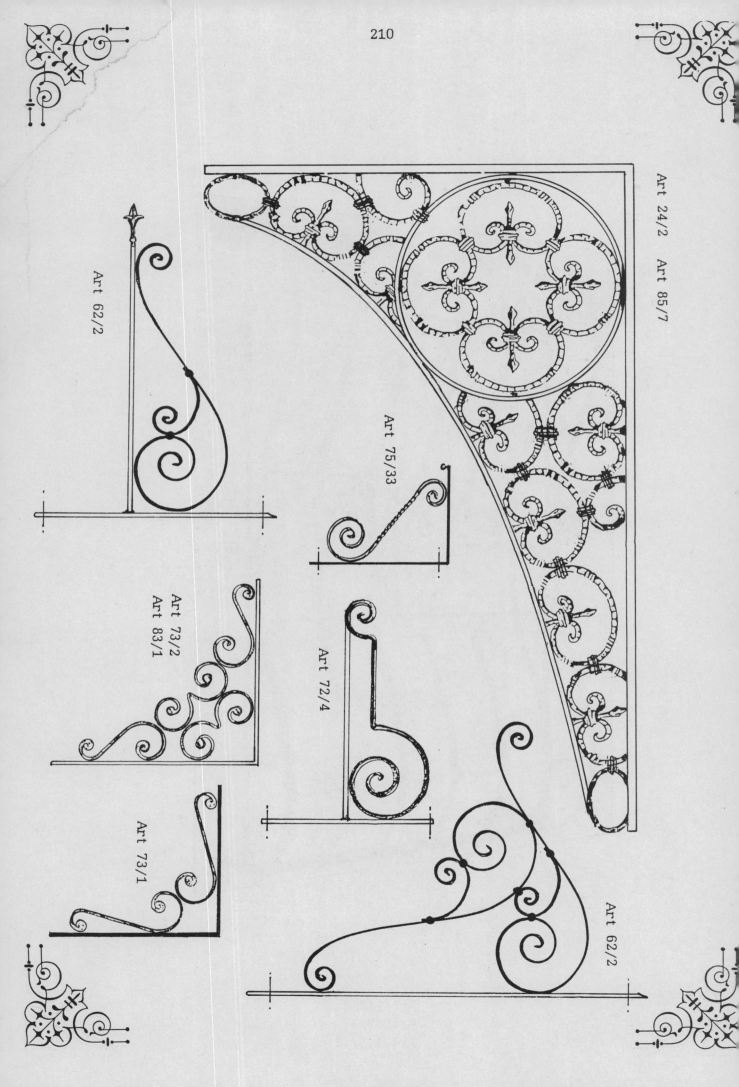

Art 24/2   Art 85/7

Art 62/2

Art 75/33

Art 73/2
Art 83/1

Art 72/4

Art 73/1

Art 62/2

Standard Sections

MILD STEEL FLATS

SIZE	KGS/M	SIZE	KGS/M
10 x 3mm	0.24	50 x 6mm	2.36
13 x 3mm	0.31	60 x 6mm	2.83
16 x 3mm	0.38	65 x 6mm	3.06
20 x 3mm	0.47	70 x 6mm	3.30
25 x 3mm	0.59	75 x 6mm	3.53
30 x 3mm	0.71	80 x 6mm	3.77
35 x 3mm	0.83	90 x 6mm	4.24
40 x 3mm	0.94	100 x 6mm	4.71
45 x 3mm	1.06	110 x 6mm	5.18
50 x 3mm	1.18	120 x 6mm	5.65
65 x 3mm	1.53	130 x 6mm	6.12
80 x 3mm	1.88	150 x 6mm	7.05
100 x 3mm	2.36	180 x 6mm	8.48
		200 x 6mm	9.42
13 x 5mm	0.51	220 x 6mm	10.36
16 x 5mm	0.63	250 x 6mm	11.78
20 x 5mm	0.78	300 x 6mm	14.13
25 x 5mm	0.98		
30 x 5mm	1.81	25 x 8mm	1.57
35 x 5mm	1.37	30 x 8mm	1.88
40 x 5mm	1.57	35 x 8mm	2.20
45 x 5mm	1.77	40 x 8mm	2.51
50 x 5mm	1.96	45 x 8mm	2.83
65 x 5mm	2.55	50 x 8mm	3.14
80 x 5mm	3.14	60 x 8mm	3.77
90 x 5mm	3.53	65 x 8mm	4.08
100 x 5mm	3.93	70 x 8mm	4.40
130 x 5mm	5.10	75 x 8mm	4.71
		80 x 8mm	5.02
13 x 6mm	0.61	90 x 8mm	5.65
16 x 6mm	0.75	100 x 8mm	6.28
20 x 6mm	0.94	130 x 8mm	8.16
25 x 6mm	1.18	150 x 8mm	9.42
30 x 6mm	1.41	180 x 8mm	11.3
35 x 6mm	1.65	200 x 8mm	12.56
40 x 6mm	1.88	250 x 8mm	15.70
45 x 6mm	2.12		

RECTANGULAR HOLLOW SECTION

SIZE	SIZE
50 x 25 x 2.00	80 x 40 x 3.20
50 x 25 x 2.60	80 x 40 x 4.00
50 x 25 x 3.00	88.9 x 38.1 x 2.60
50 x 25 x 3.20	88.9 x 38.1 x 3.20
50 x 30 x 2.50	90 x 50 x 3.60
50 x 30 x 3.00	90 x 50 x 5.00
50 x 30 x 3.20	100 x 50 x 3.00
60 x 40 x 2.50	100 x 50 x 3.20
60 x 40 x 3.00	100 x 50 x 4.00
60 x 40 x 3.20	100 x 50 x 5.00
60 x 40 x 4.00	100 x 60 x 3.60
63.5 x 38.1 x 2.50	120 x 60 x 3.60
63.5 x 38.1 x 3.20	120 x 60 x 5.00
76.2 x 76.2 x 2.50	120 x 60 x 6.30
76.2 x 38.1 x 3.20	120 x 80 x 5.00
76.2 x 50.8 x 3.20	120 x 80 x 6.30
80 x 40 x 3.00	200 x 100 x 5.00

CIRCULAR HOLLOW SECTION

26.9 x 3.20	76.1 x 3.20
33.7 x 3.20	76.1 x 4.00
33.7 x 4.00	88.9 x 3.20
42.4 x 3.20	88.9 x 4.00
48.3 x 3.20	114.3 x 3.60
60.3 x 3.20	114.3 x 5.00
	139.7 x 5.00

MILD STEEL FLATS

SIZE	KGS/M	SIZE	KGS/M
20 x 10mm	1.57	75 x 12mm	7.07
25 x 10mm	1.96	80 x 12mm	7.54
30 x 10mm	2.36	90 x 12mm	8.48
40 x 10mm	3.14	100 x 12mm	9.42
45 x 10mm	3.53	110 x 12mm	10.4
50 x 10mm	3.93	130 x 12mm	12.2
60 x 10mm	4.71	150 x 12mm	14.1
65 x 10mm	5.10	180 x 12mm	17.0
70 x 10mm	5.50	200 x 12mm	18.8
75 x 10mm	5.89	220 x 12mm	20.7
80 x 10mm	6.28	250 x 12mm	23.6
90 x 10mm	7.07	300 x 12mm	28.3
100 x 10mm	7.85		
110 x 10mm	8.64	25 x 15mm	2.94
120 x 10mm	9.42	30 x 15mm	3.53
130 x 10mm	10.2	40 x 15mm	4.71
150 x 10mm	11.8	45 x 15mm	5.30
180 x 10mm	14.1	50 x 15mm	5.89
200 x 10mm	15.7	60 x 15mm	7.07
250 x 10mm	19.6	65 x 15mm	7.65
300 x 10mm	23.6	70 x 15mm	8.24
		80 x 15mm	9.42
20 x 12mm	1.88	90 x 15mm	10.6
25 x 12mm	2.36	100 x 15mm	11.8
30 x 12mm	2.83	110 x 15mm	13.0
40 x 12mm	3.77	120 x 15mm	14.1
45 x 12mm	4.24	130 x 15mm	15.3
50 x 12mm	4.71	150 x 15mm	17.7
60 x 12mm	5.65	180 x 15mm	21.2
65 x 12mm	6.12	200 x 15mm	23.6
70 x 12mm	6.59	250 x 15mm	29.64
		300 x 15mm	35.3

SQUARE HOLLOW SECTION

SIZE	SIZE
20 x 20 x 2.00	63.5 x 63.5 x 3.20
20 x 20 x 2.50	70 x 70 x 3.00
25 x 25 x 2.00	70 x 70 x 3.20
30 x 30 x 2.50	70 x 70 x 3.60
25 x 25 x 3.00	70 x 70 x 4.00
25 x 25 x 3.20	70 x 70 x 5.00
30 x 30 x 3.20	76.2 x 76.2 x 2.60
40 x 40 x 2.00	76.2 x 76.2 x 3.20
40 x 40 x 2.50	80 x 80 x 3.60
40 x 40 x 3.00	80 x 80 x 5.00
40 x 40 x 3.20	80 x 80 x 6.30
40 x 40 x 4.00	90 x 90 x 3.20
50 x 50 x 2.50	90 x 90 x 3.60
50 x 50 x 3.00	90 x 90 x 5.00
50 x 50 x 3.20	100 x 100 x 3.20
50 x 50 x 4.00	100 x 100 x 4.00
50 x 50 x 5.00	100 x 100 x 5.00
60 x 60 x 3.00	100 x 100 x 6.30
60 x 60 x 3.20	150 x 150 x 5.00
60 x 60 x 4.00	150 x 150 x 6.30
60 x 60 x 5.00	

MILD STEEL FLATS

SIZE	KGS/M	SIZE	KGS/M
30 x 20mm	4.71	50 x 30mm	11.8
40 x 20mm	6.28	60 x 30mm	14.13
45 x 20mm	7.07	65 x 30mm	15.3
50 x 20mm	7.85	75 x 30mm	17.70
65 x 20mm	10.2	80 x 30mm	18.8
70 x 20mm	11.0	90 x 30mm	21.2
75 x 20mm	11.78	100 x 30mm	23.6
80 x 20mm	12.6	130 x 30mm	30.6
90 x 20mm	14.1	150 x 30mm	35.3
100 x 20mm	15.7		
130 x 20mm	20.4	50 x 40mm	15.7
150 x 20mm	23.6	60 x 40mm	18.84
180 x 20mm	28.3	65 x 40mm	20.4
200 x 20mm	31.4	80 x 40mm	25.1
250 x 20mm	39.25	90 x 40mm	28.3
300 x 20mm	47.1	100 x 40mm	31.4
		130 x 40mm	40.8
30 x 25mm	5.9	150 x 40mm	47.1
40 x 25mm	7.85		
45 x 25mm	8.83	75 x 50mm	25.6
50 x 25mm	9.81	80 x 50mm	31.4
60 x 25mm	9.42	100 x 50mm	39.3
65 x 25mm	12.8	130 x 50mm	51.0
70 x 25mm	13.7		
75 x 25mm	14.72		
80 x 25mm	15.7		
90 x 25mm	17.7		
100 x 25mm	19.6		
110 x 25mm	21.6		
130 x 25mm	25.5		
150 x 25mm	29.4		
180 x 25mm	35.3		
200 x 25mm	39.3		
250 x 25mm	49.06		
300 x 25mm	58.8		

MILD STEEL ROUNDS

SIZE	KGS/M	SIZE	KGS/M
6mm dia	0.22	75mm dia	34.7
8mm dia	0.39	80 mm dia	24.03
10mm dia	0.62	85mm dia	44.5
12mm dia	0.89	90mm dia	49.9
16mm dia	1.58	100mm dia	61.7
20mm dia	2.47	110mm dia	74.6
22mm dia	2.98	120mm dia	60.25
25mm dia	3.85	130mm dia	104.0
30mm dia	5.55	140mm dia	121.0
32mm dia	6.31	145mm dia	130.0
38mm dia	8.90	150mm dia	139.0
40mm dia	9.86	160mm dia	158.0
45mm dia	12.5	170mm dia	178.0
50mm dia	15.4	180mm dia	200.0
60mm dia	22.2	200mm dia	247.0
65mm dia	26.0	220mm dia	298.0
70mm dia	30.2	250mm dia	385.0

MILD STEEL SQUARES

SIZE	KGS/M	SIZE	KGS/M
10mm sq	0;78	50mm sq	19.6
13mm sq	1.33	60mm sq	28.3
16mm sq	2.01	65mm sq	33.25
20mm sq	3.14	70mm sq	38.50
22mm sq	3.80	75mm sq	44.16
25mm sq	4.91	80mm sq	50.24
30mm sq	7.07	90mm sq	63.59
40mm sq	12.60	100mm sq	78.50
45mm sq	15.9		

Conversion Tables

Fractions to decimals and mm

Fraction	Decimal	mm
1/64	0·015625	0·40
1/32	0·03125	0·79
3/64	0·046875	1·19
1/16	0·0625	1·59
5/64	0·078125	1·98
3/32	0·09375	2·38
7/64	0·109375	2·78
1/8	0·125	3·18
9/64	0·140625	3·57
5/32	0·15625	3·97
11/64	0·171875	4·37
3/16	0·1875	4·76
13/64	0·203125	5·16
7/32	0·21875	5·56
15/64	0·234375	5·95
1/4	0·25	6·35
17/64	0·265625	6·75
9/32	0·28125	7·14
19/64	0·296875	7·54
5/16	0·3125	7·94
21/64	0·328125	8·33
11/32	0·34375	8·73
23/64	0·359375	9·13
3/8	0·375	9·53
25/64	0·390625	9·92
13/32	0·40625	10·32
27/64	0·421875	10·72
7/16	0·4375	11·11
29/64	0·453125	11·51
15/32	0·46875	11·91
31/64	0·484375	12·30
1/2	0·5	12·70
33/64	0·515625	13·10
17/32	0·53125	13·49
35/64	0·546875	13·89
9/16	0·5625	14·29
37/64	0·578125	14·68
19/32	0·59375	15·08
39/64	0·609375	15·48
5/8	0·625	15·88
41/64	0·640625	16·27
21/32	0·65625	16·67
43/64	0·671875	17·07
11/16	0·6875	17·46
45/64	0·703125	17·86
23/32	0·71875	18·26
47/64	0·734375	18·65
3/4	0·75	19·05
49/64	0·765625	19·45
25/32	0·78125	19·84
51/64	0·796875	20·24
13/16	0·8125	20·64
53/64	0·828125	21·03
27/32	0·84375	21·43
55/64	0·859375	21·83
7/8	0·875	22·22
57/64	0·890625	22·62
29/32	0·90625	23·02
59/64	0·921875	23·42
15/16	0·9375	23·81
61/64	0·953125	24·21
31/32	0·96875	24·61
63/64	0·984375	25·00
1	1·0	25·40

Millimetres to inches

mm	inches	mm	inches
1	·039	65	2·559
2	·079	66	2·598
3	·118	67	2·638
4	·157	68	2·677
5	·197	69	2·717
6	·236	70	2·756
7	·276	71	2·795
8	·315	72	2·835
9	·354	73	2·874
10	·394	74	2·913
11	·433	75	2·953
12	·472	76	2·992
13	·512	77	3·031
14	·551	78	3·071
15	·591	79	3·110
16	·630	80	3·150
17	·669	81	3·189
18	·709	82	3·228
19	·748	83	3·268
20	·787	84	3·307
21	·827	85	3·346
22	·866	86	3·386
23	·906	87	3·425
24	·945	88	3·465
25	·984	89	3·504
26	1·024	90	3·543
27	1·063	91	3·583
28	1·102	92	3·622
29	1·142	93	3·661
30	1·181	94	3·701
31	1·220	95	3·740
32	1·260	96	3·780
33	1·299	97	3·819
34	1·339	98	3·858
35	1·378	99	3·898
36	1·417	100	3·937
37	1·457		
38	1·496		
39	1·535		
40	1·575		
41	1·614		
42	1·654		
43	1·693		
44	1·732		
45	1·772		
46	1·811		
47	1·850		
48	1·890		
49	1·929		
50	1·969		
51	2·008		
52	2·047		
53	2·087		
54	2·126		
55	2·165		
56	2·205		
57	2·244		
58	2·283		
59	2·323		
60	2·362		
61	2·402		
62	2·441		
63	2·480		
64	2·520		

S.w.g. Equivalents in inches and millimetres

S.w.g.	Equivalents Inches	Millimetres
1	·300	7·62
2	·276	7·01
3	·252	6·40
4	·232	5·89
5	·212	5·38
6	·192	4·88
7	·176	4·47
8	·160	4·06
9	·144	3·65
10	·128	3·25
11	·116	2·95
12	·104	2·64
13	·092	2·34
14	·080	2·03
15	·072	1·83
16	·064	1·63
17	·056	1·42
18	·048	1·22
19	·040	1·02
20	·036	·91
21	·032	·81
22	·028	·71
23	·024	·61
24	·022	·56
25	·020	·51
26	·018	·46
27	·0164	·42
28	·0148	·38
29	·0136	·35
30	·0124	·32

S.w.g. = Standard Wire Gauge.

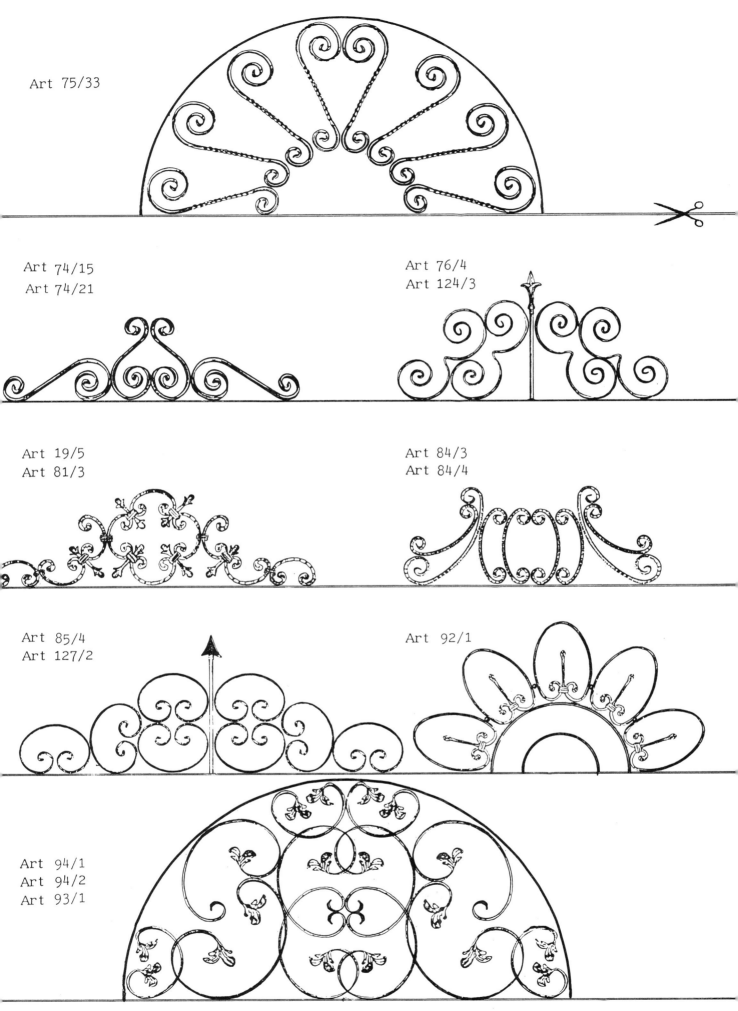

Art 75/33

Art 74/15
Art 74/21

Art 76/4
Art 124/3

Art 19/5
Art 81/3

Art 84/3
Art 84/4

Art 85/4
Art 127/2

Art 92/1

Art 94/1
Art 94/2
Art 93/1

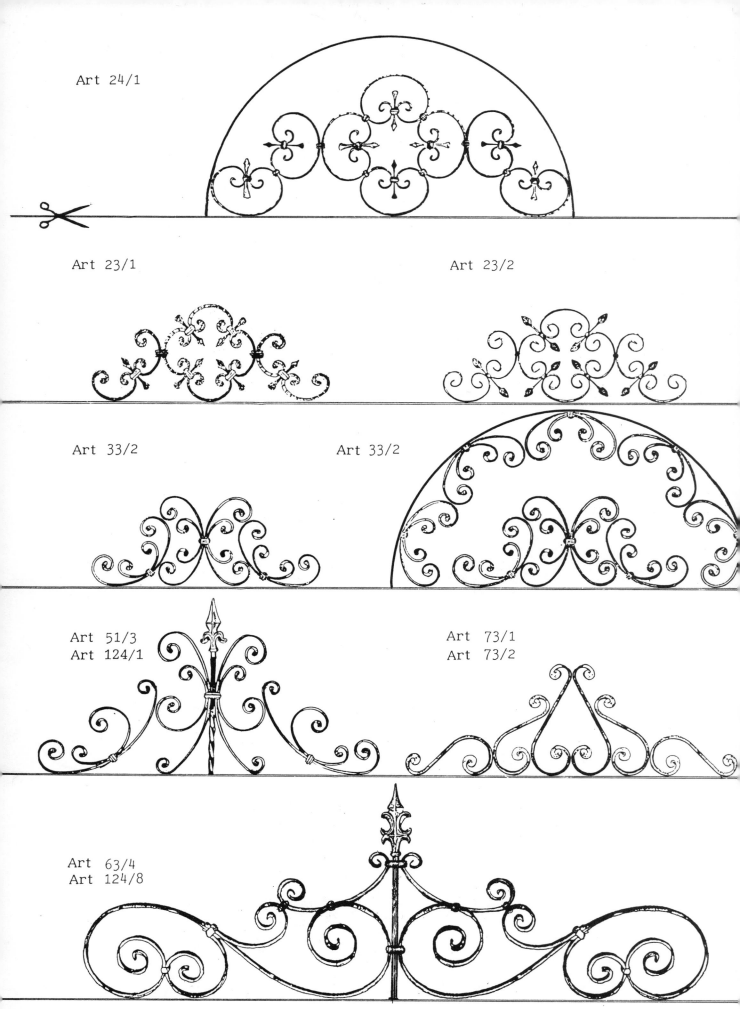

Art 24/1

Art 23/1

Art 23/2

Art 33/2

Art 33/2

Art 51/3
Art 124/1

Art 73/1
Art 73/2

Art 63/4
Art 124/8